JESUS, Help Me Pray!

JESUS, *Help Me Pray!*

BRINGING
MEANING TO THE
Lord's Prayer

ANGELA ACKLEY

6-WEEK BIBLE STUDY
(Online Videos Included)

Xulon Press
2301 Lucien Way #415
Maitland, FL 32751
407.339.4217
www.xulonpress.com

Printed in the United States of America

Paperback ISBN-13: 978-1-66283-615-2
Ebook ISBN-13: 978-1-66283-616-9

Dedication

This Bible study is dedicated to Ashley Jacobs. I have kept Ashley at the front of my mind throughout the writing of this study. Ashley and I met at a coffee shop in April of 2019. At the end of our conversation we joined hands and I prayed for her. After the prayer, she looked at me with tears in her eyes and said, "Can you teach me how to pray?" My spirit burned within me and I knew that somehow and some way God was going to lead me to teach people how to pray.

Table of Contents

Introduction

Prayer means "asking God for something." Right?

We all have questions about prayer. How do I pray? Why should I pray? What's the point of prayer? When I first became a Christian I was so put off by praying. I did not see the point of making a list of prayers and praying them day after day after day until they were answered. It seemed repetitive and quite frankly...boring. And poor God. If I was tired of *saying* my list, I couldn't imagine how tired He must be of *listening* to it! I just didn't see the point of repeating my wishes until I was blue in the face, hoping He would answer so I could finally cross one thing off my list. I felt that if I didn't pray enough, it was my fault that my prayers were not getting answered.

After talking to many people, I am completely convinced that when people hear the word "pray", they define it as "ask God for something." When people are sick, we say that we will pray and ask God to heal them. When people are traveling, we say that we will pray and ask God to protect them. When we want a new job, we ask God to help us find a new job. If we need money, we ask God to give us money. For many people, that is their prayer life: asking God for something. This definition of prayer made me feel fully responsible if my prayers were answered or not. The whole thing just didn't make sense and left me feeling like I was ultimately in charge of my prayers being answered.

Now, I am *not* saying that we shouldn't ask God for stuff. We absolutely should. James 4:2 says "you do not have because you do not ask God." Part of prayer is asking for things (and being bold in your asking). What I *am* saying is that there is WAY more to prayer than just asking. If we redefine prayer—change it from "asking God for something" to "building and fostering a relationship with God"—everything about prayer changes.

I want you to stop and think for a moment about that idea of having a relationship with God. Do you have that one friend who just won't stop talking? You know the one who when you see her name come up on your phone, you contemplate if you should answer, knowing that it's going to be a good hour of listening??? The one who does not let you get a word in edgewise and then interrupts you when you finally get to say something? Have you identified her? Let's be real: she may be a friend of yours, but those one-way conversations get old and can leave you feeling like she doesn't even care about what's going on in your life. I bring this up because sometimes we can be like this with God. We can talk, talk, talk at God without even taking a breath before we say "Amen". It almost goes without saying, but those kinds of conversations are not great relationship-building conversations. Just like a healthy conversation with another person, we want to talk to God, but then give Him space to speak to our heart about something. Prayer is really a two-way communication. We should always be ready and willing to hear God speak during prayer.

When we change our definition of prayer, we start to get to know Him instead of only asking from Him. We start to understand how He works and we begin to see the world through His eyes, which in this day and age is invaluable! When we build a relationship with the Father, we begin to have a friend who we can talk to at ANY time, night or day. When we want to talk to our Father in heaven, He is never out of the office, on vacation, or too tired to talk. He is always available.

And how about building a relationship with the wisest person in the universe? God has all the wisdom in the world because He created everything. He knows exactly how everything works. Asking God questions in prayer is a great way to know what He thinks and how things work. So many times when we run into a struggle, the first thing we think to do is make a phone call to a friend, family member, or co-worker. But do we remember that God has the PERFECT answer?

Throughout this Bible study on the Lord's Prayer, I hope that you will see that we not only ask God for things in prayer, but we also build a relationship with Him that will impact every part of our lives. You will also see, as we study this passage of Scripture, that the Lord's Prayer gives us a structure to pray: we look **upward** as we praise God, we look **outward** as we pray for others, we look **inward** as we pray for ourselves, we learn how to **confess**, and finally we learn how to pray **protection.**

After every day of study, I've added a prayer in italics. When you come to the end of each day of study, please pray the prayer out loud. There is power in speaking prayers out loud! In addition to speaking prayers out loud, it is also powerful to pray our prayers *in Jesus' name*. When we pray *in Jesus' name,* we are praying with the authority and power given to us in Jesus!

Here's our first prayer to get us started. Join me in saying this prayer out loud:

Father, as we dive into this study on the Lord's Prayer, I pray that the Word of God would come alive. I pray that You would prepare our hearts for what You are about to speak. Light a fire in our hearts to want to know more about You and the power of prayer. Lord, I am asking that by the end of this study, we would have a deeper understanding of You and that we would have a deeper intimacy with You. Father, teach us how to pray and bring Your revelation! In Jesus' name, Amen.

Week One

Our Father who art in heaven, hallowed by Your name,

Look Upward!

Video One

(To watch Video One, go to angelaackley.com)

Watch Video One and use this space to take notes. You may want to jot down any Scriptures that speak to you or any comments or stories that you don't want to forget!

_____

_____

_____

_____

_____

_____

_____

_____

_____

_____

_____

_____

_____

_____

_____

_____

_____

_____

_____

_____

This week we will be looking **upward** and will be learning how to praise God through our prayers.

Day 1

GOD IN HEAVEN

"Our Father who art in heaven, hallowed be Your name" – Matthew 6:9

One morning I was on my knees doing my daily prayers and I happened to start out with the Lord's Prayer. I don't do that every morning, but I did it this particular morning. The first line struck me in a way that it had never struck me before. *Our Father who art in heaven.* Wait a minute. God never comes out of heaven? So many times I feel Him, I sense Him, I am comforted by Him. I feel so close to Him, yet God never leaves heaven. Wow. It was one of those moments where God revealed yet another detail about Himself through the simple act of spending time with Him.

Let's spend some time now looking at how Scripture describes God in heaven. Read the following passages and list the details describing God and His surroundings:

Isaiah 6:1-4

_____

_____

_____

Ezekiel 1:25-28

_____

_____

_____

Revelation 4:2-6

_____

_____

_____

These three passages give us a picture of our Father in heaven. Many times we picture God as a little old man sitting in a rocking chair, but these three descriptions blow that picture out of the water. God is not human. He doesn't think like we think. He doesn't act like we act. If we are going to believe that "with God nothing will be impossible" (Luke 1:37, NKJV), we need to replace the little-old-man image with the truth of who He is, as shown in His Word. Read each passage again and allow yourself to picture "Our Father who art in heaven."

Describe the scene in each passage of Scripture:

Isaiah 6:1-4

_____

_____

_____

Ezekiel 1:25-28

_____

_____

_____

Revelation 4:2-6

_____

_____

_____

As you allow the details to come together and give you a picture of our Father in heaven, spend a couple minutes envisioning the scene.

This scene is a wonderful way to enter into prayer with Him. As we enter into prayer, we need to be reminded that God is not confined to a box with rules and hindrances. We need to be reminded that He is capable of the impossible, capable of miracles, and capable of keeping everything from falling apart. We need to know that we serve a God who created the universe and everything in it.

Have you ever stopped to think about some of God's creations? About how creative He is or how He just doesn't think like humans think? Take animals, for example. Have you ever stopped and thought about a rhinoceros? I'm just going to say it: they are the weirdest-looking animals. If I don't stop and think *How creative!*, I might just go to *God, what were you thinking?!* God, in His creativity and marvel, created giraffes with unthinkably long necks and elephants with unthinkably long noses, dolphins with special skin to glide through the water and a special thing inside woodpeckers' heads so they don't get a headache when they are pecking away on a tree trunk. Is there anything that He has not thought of?

The point I'm trying to make here is that when we enter into the presence of God through prayer, we need to enter into a place of awe and wonder. We need to know that we are talking to THE

GOD OF THE UNIVERSE, not a little old man in a box. We need to know that He is large and in charge and that we are not. We need to know that He is more than capable and He is not of this world. He is bigger than this world and the problems that often consume us. He can take our small little problems and fix them in a way that we had never even thought of.

OK, now that we know who we are talking to, it's time to enter into His presence!

Father, You are amazing and creative and majestic. Thank You for the small glimpses we get of You through Scripture. Blow our minds with how long, how high, how deep, and how wide Your love is for us. Show us who You are! Show us Your majesty! We adore You! In Jesus' name, Amen.

Reflection, Notes or Prayer

Day 2

ENTER INTO THE CAVE

"Our Father in heaven, hallowed be Your name" –
Matthew 6:9

A couple of months ago, I was invited to speak at a three-day silent retreat. Sounds kind of like an oxymoron, I know (speaking at a silent retreat?!), but I was asked to give a message that would usher the women into silence for that night and the next day, and then to break the silence on the third day. As I was preparing, it became clear that God wanted me to share on the topic of *Praising God.* He reminded me of a local cave that I had recently visited called Cave of the Mounds. This Wisconsin cave is a natural National Landmark and is more than a million years old! Cave of the Mounds is unique in that no bats or typical cave creatures dwell there. Incredibly, it is also exactly 50 degrees year-round no matter what is happening above the surface. Heat waves, snowstorms, tornados, etc. have absolutely no effect on the temperature of the cave. Nothing above ground makes this cave change.

In showing me the picture of this cave, God was also showing me that when we enter His presence through prayer, we are entering His cave where He is exactly the same yesterday, today, and forever. He doesn't change based on the storms or the circumstances in our lives. When we come into His presence, we are not going to be annoyed by the critters and pests that are flying around us, trying to distract us and get us off track. When we come to Him, we enter into a place of peace and tranquility that is free of distraction and is unchanging. We enter into the cave with God.

Psalm 46:1-3 says, *"God is our refuge and strength, an ever-present help in trouble. Therefore we will not fear, though the earth give way and the mountains fall into the heart of the sea, though its waters roar and foam and the mountains quake with their surging."*

This Psalm perfectly describes God's cave for us! Even though it feels like the earth is giving way around us and the mountains are falling into the sea, God is our refuge and our strength when everything seems to be falling apart!

After finishing the message for the silent retreat, I was closing my laptop when the Lord spoke to me: *I did my best work in a cave.* Whoa! I was not expecting that, but oh boy, did He ever! Jesus was dead and placed in a cave Friday night through Saturday and rose from the dead on Sunday. Yes, I would have to agree: God did His best work in a cave. Let's do what Jesus did and enter into a cave with God. He may just resurrect some dead things within us!

Spend some time imagining God from yesterday's lesson. Now imagine being in a cave with God where there are no distractions, where there is peace, and where the circumstances of your life are not weighing on you. Sit with Him and don't talk. Just be still. Practice sitting with God in a cave this week. "Be still, and know that I am God" (Psalm 46:10).

Father, Your presence is powerful. Thank You for allowing us to be in Your presence. Thank You for speaking to our hearts and removing all the distractions around us. Thank You that You are our refuge and our strength and that You are unchanging. You are the same yesterday, today, and forever. In Jesus' name, Amen.

Reflection, Notes or Prayer

_____

_____

_____

_____

_____

_____

_____

_____

DAY 2

Day 3

ENTERING THE CAVE BY PRAISING GOD

"Our Father in heaven, hallowed be Your name" –
Matthew 6:9

My mom, who will be 71 this year, has been following Jesus Christ since she was eight years old. A bus used to pick her up every Sunday for church as a child and that is where she met God. She loves Him with her whole heart and He has been her Father ever since. When I first talked to her about starting prayer with praising God, she didn't really understand what I was saying. Don't get me wrong; my mom thanks God every day (for everything!) and talks to God all day long, but the concept of praising God was a new one for her. I mention this only because if it's a new concept for my mom, who has been a Christian for almost 63 years, it may be a new concept for you as well.

Now I know that talking about praising God might be a tough concept right out of the gate, but stick with me. It's really the most important part of developing our relationship with God. This topic can seem obscure and difficult to grasp, so I am going to lay it out as simply as I can. God moves mountains when we praise Him!

Let me take one step back. What does "praising" God mean? When Jesus teaches us how to pray, He starts out by saying, "Our Father, who art in heaven, *hallowed be Your name*" (emphasis mine). If you are like me, you have said these words out loud many times, but have never really known what the word "hallowed" means. Well, "hallowed" means greatly revered, sacred, and holy.[1] Jesus teaches us to greatly revere and honor our holy God. When we pray His praises back to God, we don't ask Him for anything. We don't come to Him with our list. Quite frankly, praising God has absolutely nothing to do with us. Praising God is all about who HE is. It's all about worshipping, honoring, and revering HIM.

When my husband and I first began praying together, we would start our time praising God together. After a couple of weeks of praying together, we had just finished a walk and were sitting on a bench overlooking a little pond when my husband said, "Can I ask you a question? And I don't want you to get upset." (OK now, if you are married, you know to brace yourself for what is coming!) He knows how passionate I am about prayer, so he was obviously treading lightly. He continued, "How come when we are in our praise time, you go on and on and on? Don't you think that God is up there thinking, *Enough already! I know who I am, you don't need to remind Me. Let's get to the real business!*" I let out a sigh of relief and was actually so grateful that he asked this question. If my own husband asked this question, I'm sure that there are others out there asking the same thing!

Here's the thing. We don't praise God because He needs to know who He is or because He is insecure or because He wants us to build Him up or butter Him up. No. God is totally secure in who He is. God does not need us to praise Him. *Praising God is for us.* It's so WE can be reminded of WHO HE IS. We get so wrapped up in our world and in our circumstances that we forget who He is and that nothing is impossible for Him. We put Him in a box. We need to praise Him to remind us to let Him out of the box!

If you are still asking yourself what the big deal is about praising God first in your prayer time, here is a recap. When we begin by praising God and reminding ourselves who God is—*Our Father who art in heaven, hallowed be your name*—we are ushered into the presence of God. Praising God takes us into the cave with God where the circumstances and storms of life are dulled and where we are reminded that God is bigger and more powerful than any issue in our lives. It prepares our minds for the things we need to ask for and for the people we are about to pray for. It's much different to ask for things or to pray for people when you are in a mindset that nothing is impossible for God. Our prayers tend to get bigger and we become more bold and confident in what we ask. We begin to know God's personality and how He works, and our prayers become more and more in alignment with His will.

There's another advantage to praising God daily in our prayer time. When we practice praising God on a daily basis, it becomes a tool that we can use when tragedy strikes. (And it will. The Bible declares it.) Praising God gets our mind off our problems and helps remind us who is in control and can solve our problems. Here is the tool of "praise" at work in my life recently.

One of our boys was getting a talking-to from my husband. We had just found out something that we needed to address. I was pretty upset at the recent revelation, so instead of going downstairs and joining in the conversation, I sat in my room and praised God for 45 minutes of the hour-long conversation. Now, it would have been easy to sit in my room and fixate on the problem at hand, allowing my mind to go down the bunny trail and worry about every scenario that *could* happen. But I knew I had another option, a better option: To praise God in the midst of unfavorable circumstances. To remind myself of who God is and what He can do. And guess what? Fear and anxiety never took root. I was able to get through what we needed to get through without being debilitated by fear and anxiety. Many times in the Bible, we are shown that praising God moves mountains. For example, the walls of Jericho fell because God's people faithfully walked around the walls worshipping and praising the Lord. When Paul and Silas were in prison, they began to sing hymns to the Lord and a violent earthquake shook the earth and their chains became loose and they were freed.

So now that we know what praising God means, how do we do it? There are several ways that we can start our prayer time by praising God.

1. The first way we can praise God is through worship music. This is by far one of the easiest and quickest ways to enter into the presence of God. Whether you put in a pair of earbuds to play your Worship playlist or you ask Alexa to play praise and worship music, worship music can powerfully usher us into the presence of God.

   Now I want to stop here and say that not all Christian music is created the same when it comes to wanting to enter the presence of God. Christian pop music is not exactly what we are looking for here. Most of Christian pop music is about "us" or "me"...about what *I* am experiencing, what *I* am hoping for, and how *I* feel. While this type of music can surely minister to our hearts, we are looking for music that is all about *God* during the "Praising God" part of our prayer time.

I would suggest creating a Worship playlist and then add just the Christian songs that are truly worshipping God and focusing on God. The other Christian music is great to listen to, just not during the praise part of our prayer time. (If you are looking for worship music suggestions, please visit my website at www.angelaackley.com.)

This method of listening to worship music may not challenge us to dig into Scripture or think about His attributes, but it does usher us very quickly into His presence. The next five methods for praising God through prayer will take time, patience, learning, and being still with Him, all of which really develop the intimacy and relationship with God that we are searching for.

2. **The second way we can praise God is by praying His names back to Him.** In a prayer group that I led recently, while we were praising God, we spent about 15 minutes just praying the names of God or words that describe Him. Now that's a long time for one-word names, but we just kept coming up with more and more names and words to describe Him. It was wonderful! One thing that I've done for years is keep a page in my journal just for names or words that describe God. When I'm reading through the Bible and come across a name or description of God, I write it in my specially-designated journal page and then pray those words or names back to God during my praise time.

Just to get you started, I'm going to name a few of what I'm talking about:

Healer, I Am, Messiah, Yahweh, Prince of Peace, The Spotless Lamb, Faithful, Forgiving, Friend, Our Refuge, The Way The Truth and The Life, God Almighty, The Word became Flesh, Ancient of Days, Love, Our Stronghold, Comforter, Helper, Advocate, Protector, Jesus, Our Father.

As you meditate on who He is, allow the Holy Spirit to bring names and words that describe Him to your mind. Go ahead and do that right now and write down any that pop into your mind even if I have them listed above. If you can't think of any, go ahead and use our friend Google for help!

3. **The third way we praise God is by learning and praying God's attributes and His character.** I think that this step is so very important, but also very challenging. If we are going to pray God's attributes, we need to know what His attributes are, but it's not a subject that we talk about a whole lot. When we challenge ourselves to learn about God and His attributes, it helps us to go deeper into who God really is. So how do we learn about God's character and His attributes? By spending time with Him. To help you get started, I'm going to have you answer some questions:

Think about how much God cares for us. What are some words that come to your mind? List them (e.g., love, compassion, friend, comforter, provider, helper).

_____

_____

Think about how God leads us. What are some words that come to your mind? List them (e.g., counselor, wisdom, shepherd).

_____

_____

_____

Think about how good God is. What are some words that describe His goodness? List them (e.g., mercy, grace, love, holiness, peace, righteous, perfect).

_____

_____

_____

Think about how big God is. What are some words that describe how big He is? List them (e.g., creator of the universe, of human life, of animals and of atoms, omnipresent, omniscient).

_____

_____

_____

When we start to search out God and learn about Him, we discover new traits and attributes about Him and we begin to understand His heart for His people, and more specifically for us, and more specifically for you and for me.

In our praise time to God, we can simply list off His attributes and His character traits back to Him. Such a great way to remind ourselves of who He is and to go deeper with Him as we search out who He is.

4. **The fourth way of praising God is taking step 3 one step further.** Take the names and attributes of God that you have listed in step 3 and **choose one to meditate on**. For example, if I chose *Healer*, I would sit with God and pray back to Him all the ways He is the *Healer*.

For example:

Father, thank You for being our Healer. Thank You for creating the human body, our souls, and our spirits. Thank You that You know exactly what needs to be healed and You know exactly how to do it. You made the human body and understand things about our bodies that even the best doctors in the world do not understand. I praise You for Your knowledge and understanding of such things. I praise You for knowing things about us that we don't even know about ourselves. I praise You for shining Your light on the dark places in our hearts and healing us. You are amazing and brilliant and all-knowing. We praise You as our Healer.

Scriptures on Healing:

Exodus 15:26 *"for I am the Lord, who heals you."*

Acts 4:30 (NLT) *"Stretch out Your hand with healing power, may miraculous signs and wonders be done through the name of your holy servant Jesus."*

Do you see how as you pray these things back to Him, you are reminded of who He is and how wonderful and capable He is???

Wow, friends! You have worked SO hard today. Remember, this first verse of the Lord's Prayer is the most challenging one and it's only going to get easier from here. Praising God is one of the most important parts of our prayer time so even though it's hard, your work will pay off. Join me back here tomorrow for the last two methods for praising God. It's going to be worth every minute!

Father, I thank You that You love us so much that You teach us how to pray. I thank You that You are teaching us more and more about You through praising You. Thank You that You give us the tool of praise to help us remind ourselves who You are. Open up our spiritual eyes and ears so that we can understand You more! We want to know You more! In Jesus' name, Amen.

Reflection, Notes or Prayer

Day 4

"Our Father in heaven, hallowed be Your name" –
Matthew 6:9

STILL PRAISING GOD

5. The fifth way we are going to learn to praise God is through the "ABCs of Praise." This method of praise takes everything that we have learned about praising God up to this point and melts it all together. Basically, just start at the beginning of the alphabet and think of words that either describe God or are a name of God and continue through the alphabet.

Go ahead and try it now (e.g., A=awesome, able; B=beautiful, bountiful, big; C=comforter, caring).

_____

_____

_____

_____

_____

6. The sixth and final method for praising God is reading the Psalms. I've chosen six Psalms in particular that I believe help us worship, praise, and revere God.

Open your Bibles and read the listed Psalms. As you read each one, write down different character traits or attributes about God. Remember, our goal is to praise God for who He is. Write down the things that describe who He is so that you can pray these things back to Him. I will do the first two for you.

Psalm 113

Write down the main messages of Psalm 113:

Praise the Lord! The Lord is exalted over all the nations, His glory above the heavens, no one is like our Lord, He is the One who sits enthroned on high, He stoops down to look on the heavens and earth, He raises the poor from dust, lifts the needy from the ash heap, He seats the poor with princes, He gives childless women children.

Write the attributes (descriptions) of God in Psalm 113:

Exalted, Glorious, the one and only God, sits on His throne, sees the heavens and the earth, raises the poor and needy, provides.

Write a prayer (using what you wrote above) for Psalm 113:

We praise You, Lord! You are lifted high. You are exalted over all the nations. There is no nation or tribe above You. No one is like You, Lord. You are the one and only true God. You are seated in the highest heaven on the highest throne. No one is seated above You. You are so high that You have to stoop down to look at the heavens and the earth beneath You. Your eye is on the poor. Your desire is to raise up the poor and the needy. You lift up the poor and needy and give them what You desire.

Psalm 138

Write down the main messages of Psalm 138:

I will praise You with my whole heart! I will sing Your praise. I will bow down to You. I will praise You for Your unfailing love and faithfulness. You answer when I call and give me courage. May all the kings praise You. Though the Lord is exalted, He sees the lowly. Though I walk in trouble, You preserve my life. You save me with Your right hand. You clear me of blame and Your love endures forever!

Write the attributes (descriptions) of God in Psalm 138:

Unfailing love, faithful, giver of courage, glorious, exalted, looks kindly on the lowly, sees the lowly from afar, preserves life, stretches out His hand in anger, protector, savior, vindicates, loving.

Write a prayer (using what you wrote above) for Psalm 138:

Father, I praise You with my whole heart and I sing Your praises. I bow down to You and praise You for Your unfailing love and faithfulness. You answer when I call and You give me courage. May all the kings of the earth praise You. You are exalted and You see me. You see me when I walk in trouble and You preserve my life and You save me with Your right hand! You clear me of blame and Your love endures forever. You are loving and faithful. You give me courage and are glorious. You are my protector, my savior, and my vindicator. I praise You for Your love!

Psalm 139

Write down the main messages of Psalm 139:

_____

_____

_____

Write the attributes (descriptions) of God in Psalm 139:

_____

_____

_____

Write a prayer (using what you wrote above) for Psalm 139:

_____

_____

_____

Psalm 145

Write down the main messages of Psalm 145:

_____

_____

_____

Write the attributes (descriptions) of God in Psalm 145:

_____

_____

_____

Write a prayer (using what you wrote above) for Psalm 145:

_____

_____

Psalm 148

Write down the main messages of Psalm 148:

_____

_____

Write the attributes (descriptions) of God in Psalm 148:

_____

_____

Write a prayer (using what you wrote above) for Psalm 148:

_____

_____

Psalm 150

Write down the main messages of Psalm 150:

_____

_____

_____

Write the attributes (descriptions) of God in Psalm 150:

_____

_____

_____

Write a prayer (using what you wrote above) for Psalm 150:

_____

_____

_____

Isn't this fun?! I love the Psalms. If you are short on time, another way you can use the Psalms as part of your praise time is to have them read to you. My husband and I, before we start our prayer time together, will ask Alexa to read us a particular Psalm or two. The spoken Word is powerful and is another way we can connect with God.

We made it through our week of praising God. Unseen (and seen) things happen when we praise God! Pick one of the six methods of praise that we have been studying and dive in. Once you feel like you have mastered one, go to another or rotate every day. Learn them however you want, but please give each one a try. Your intimacy with God will grow and you will enter into the presence of God like never before. As I write this, our family is going through some dark days of uncertainty. Praising God has gotten us through this! If we practice praising God when things are going well, we are prepared to praise God when things aren't going so well. I can't wait to see what God is going to show you. Blessings to you, my sweet friends! Now onto week 2 and the second verse of the Lord's prayer!

Father, thank You for helping us through this week of learning how to praise You. Thank You for teaching us a new way to pray. Thank You that You are showing us how to take our eyes off ourselves and place our eyes on You. You are amazing and we praise You! In Jesus' name, Amen.

Reflection, Notes or Prayer

_____

_____

_____

_____

_____

_____

_____

_____

_____

_____

Week Two

Your kingdom come, Your will be done, on earth as it is in heaven.

Look Outward!

Video Two

(To watch *Video Two*, go to angelaackley.com)

Watch Video Two and use this space to take notes. You may want to jot down any Scriptures that speak to you or any comments or stories that you don't want to forget!

_____

_____

_____

_____

_____

_____

_____

_____

_____

_____

_____

_____

_____

_____

_____

_____

_____

_____

_____

This week we will be looking **outward** and focusing on praying for others.

Day 1

"Your kingdom come, Your will be done, on earth as it is in heaven." – Matthew 6:10

YOUR KINGDOM COME

Of all the verses in the Lord's Prayer, this one has always been the most confusing for me. Can you relate? When God gave me clarity on it, there was a true shift for the better in my prayer life. Here we go!

Your kingdom come, Your will be done on earth as it is in heaven. Truly, this is a life-changing verse when we really understand it, so I'm going to do my best to pull it apart for you. First of all, did you know that when God created the earth, He called it perfect and good? God's original plan for earth was to be perfect like it is in heaven. Can you imagine that?

The earth was perfect and good for the first two chapters of Genesis (the first book of the Bible). Then something horrible happened. In Genesis, chapter 3, sin entered the world and sin has exponentially grown over time. (Please read Genesis chapters 1-3 if you haven't done so recently.) We now live in a very broken world with sin running rampant. My point here is that ORIGINALLY the earth was like heaven. When sin entered, a gap was created between heaven and earth. It's in this gap that God asks us to pray.

In the white space below, draw a heart and label it "**HEAVEN (God's perfect will)**.". Leave about an inch of space underneath the heart and draw a circle and label it "**Earth**." In the inch of space between the heart (heaven) and the circle (earth), write, "**GAP created by sin between what God wanted for the earth and what was happening on the earth**."

This **gap** is demonstrated in Ezekiel 22:30. Write the Scripture here:

Ezekiel 22:30

_____

_____

God is looking for someone to <u>stand in the gap</u> and pray for God's perfect will to be done on earth as it is in heaven! Boy, that statement can really change the course of our prayer life. Jennifer Kennedy Dean, a scholar on prayer, says it a different way. She says, "When we pray, we reach into the spiritual realm (heaven) and grab hold of the will of God for that situation. Then we pull the will of God through the gap and establish it on the earth."[2] That's so good! When we pray, we grab hold of God's will and bring it to earth!

We ask and we plead, but do we ever ask and plead for *His will* to be done? Do we trust that His plans and thoughts are higher than our plans and thoughts? Do we ever take the time and try to see our circumstances from a heavenly perspective?

One of my favorite quotes from Jennifer Kennedy Dean is, **"What God wants to do on the earth, He will do through intercessors. Prayer releases the will of God, bringing His will out of the spiritual realm and causing it to take effect in the material realm. When God wants to change the course events will take on their own, He calls out an intercessor."**[3]

For those of you who have never heard the word *intercessor* before, it means "the act of intervening between different parties, particularly the act of praying to God on behalf of another person.[4] What Jennifer is saying is this: There is a natural course events will take on their own, but God calls his people to pray to *change* the natural course of events.

I love this!! God invites us to pray so that HIS perfect will in heaven is done on earth and He invites us to partner with Him to accomplish His will here on earth. When we don't pray, the natural course of events will likely take place.

Let me try and explain with this example. I have a chaplain friend who describes going into hospital rooms of people that are very sick. If she walks into a room where there are no believers, there is very little hope because the natural course of events will probably take place. But if she walks into a room where there are believers, they can call on God to impart His power into the hopeless situation. Prayer ushers in the presence of God and the atmosphere in the room changes. God brings hope. His peace settles over us when we pray that His will be done.

Father, thank You for opening up our eyes to the power of prayer. You ask us to agree with You in prayer for Your will to come to earth. Thank You that You are looking for someone to stand in the gap between heaven and earth. Thank You that You trust us enough to use us to accomplish Your plans! In Jesus' name, Amen.

Reflection, Notes or Prayer

Day 2

"Your kingdom come, Your will be done, on earth as it is in heaven." – Matthew 6:10

PRAYING GOD'S WILL

I've led many prayer groups over the years. At one point, I had invited a friend to join one of the prayer groups I was leading and she politely declined saying that the only prayer she ever prays is for God's will to be done. Huh? On one hand it made perfect sense. We DO want God's will to be done in all circumstances, but on the other hand, what about the passages of Scripture that say, "You don't have because you don't ask"? And what about all of the Scriptures exhorting people to pray about everything and pray unceasingly, or about Jesus teaching His disciples how to pray? Yes, we need to pray for God's will to be done. After all, Jesus tells us to pray this way in the Lord's Prayer! But we need to be praying for His will to be done and so much more! We need to pray God's will, but we can't just stop there!

What my friend said about only praying God's will really forced me to dig into Scripture and prayer and to seek revelation from God. As I've spent time on this subject, I've come to the following conclusion: When we are praying for God's will to be done on earth as it is in heaven, our heart needs to be postured towards God. What I mean by this is that when we are asking for stuff or when we are praying for specific answers to prayer, our hearts need to be open to the fact that God's will "wins." We need to come to God in our prayers with a heart that is already surrendered to His will. He wants us to ask and to pray and to come boldly to His throne with requests, but the POSTURE of our heart needs to remain humble.

The *posture* of our heart when we pray needs to be:

1. **HUMBLE**: *I am asking for _____, but I understand that my ways are not Your ways so if this is not in Your will, I humbly submit my request to Your will.*

   Example of a *humbled* heart: Imagine your child (sibling, coworker) wants something from you. They know that you have the authority and means to give it to them. They ask boldly, but they humbly know that the answer may be no. When you say no, they accept the "no" and trust that you know best.

Example of a *stubborn* heart: Imagine your child (sibling, coworker) wants something from you. They know that you have the authority and means to give it to them so they proceed to DEMAND that you give it to them. They use a demanding tone mixed with anger to try and intimidate you to get what they want. *But because they are too young to understand or they don't have the information that you have access to*, you choose NOT to give them their request. You know that giving them what they want will not be good for them in the long run. They become very angry and pouty and they hold a grudge against you.

2. **SURRENDERED**: *I am asking for _____, but I understand that I am not in control and that You, God, are in __complete__ control.*

3. **WITH AUTHORITY**: *I am boldly and confidently coming to Your Throne to ask _____, but I understand that Your authority supersedes my authority.*

God says in James 4:2b that "you do not have because you do not ask God." He tells us to ask. Hebrews 4:16 says: "Let us then approach God's throne of grace with confidence, so that we may receive mercy and find grace to help us in our time of need." God wants us to ask and He wants us to approach Him with the confidence that He can accomplish what we ask, but even so, our heart needs to be in a position of submission and humility to Him. We ask; we don't demand or tell Him what to do. We ask boldly and confidently for Him to impart His power to the situation we are praying about.

We must come to God in our prayers with a humble and surrendered heart. We need to understand that He is the supreme power and authority. If we don't consider the sovereignty (supreme power and authority) of God, we can be praying our will instead of God's will. Let me explain. Let's say you've been asked to pray for someone with terminal cancer. We *do* know that God's will always is to heal someone 100%. Remember, God originally created the world to be perfect, with no sin. But we can sometimes ignore or forget the fact that *sometimes* God's perfect healing doesn't come on earth, but it comes on the other side (in heaven). Did you get that? Sometimes our healing comes on earth, but sometimes healing comes the minute we reach heaven. So, when praying for the friend with terminal cancer, we can and should pray for healing, but our sovereign God gets to choose whether the healing happens on earth or in heaven. When praying for people, we need to have a humbled and surrendered heart that yearns for God's will to be done so we make sure we aren't hurting anyone by making promises that aren't in accordance with His will.

When we open our prayer time with praise and worship of our Father and come into His presence with a heart that is humble and fully surrendered to Him, our prayers begin to align with God's will and God's heart and we start to see things as the Father sees them. And in turn, we start to pray as He would have us pray!

Sounds easy, right? No, it's not easy. Especially when we see people facing hard things, like cancer, financial stress or a crumbling marriage, addiction or job loss. How do we know what God's will is when things seem to be falling apart all around us? Well, we may not know God's exact will, but we **do** know some things about God:

We know that God's heart is good:

James 1:17 *Every good and perfect gift is from above, coming down from the Father of the heavenly lights, who does not change like shifting shadows.*

Jeremiah 29:11 *For I know the plans for you, declares the LORD, plans to prosper you and not to harm you, plans to give you hope and a future.*

Psalm 34:8 *Taste and see that the Lord is good; blessed is the one who takes refuge in Him.*

Psalm 107:1 *Give thanks to the LORD, for He is good; His love endures forever.*

Psalm 145:9 *The Lord is good to all; He has compassion on all He has made.*

Romans 8:28 *And we know that in all things God works for the good of those who love Him, who have been called according to His purpose.*

We know that God can be trusted:

1 John 1:5 *This is the message we have heard from Him and declare to you: God is light; in Him there is no darkness at all.*

Joshua 1:9 *Have I not commanded you? Be strong and courageous. Do not be afraid; do not be discouraged, for the Lord your God will be with you wherever you go.*

Psalm 9:10 *Those who know Your name trust in You, for You, Lord have never forsaken those who seek You.*

Daniel 6:23 *The king was overjoyed and gave orders to lift Daniel out of the den. And when Daniel was lifted from the den, no wound was found on him, because he had trusted in his God.*

We know that God LOVES us:

John 3:16 *For God so loved the world that He gave His one and only Son, that whoever believes in Him shall not perish but have eternal life.*

1 John 4:16 *And so we know and rely on the love God has for us. God is love. Whoever lives in love lives in God, and God in them.*

When we know that God's heart is good, that He can be trusted, and that He loves us, we can trust that God is doing good behind all the bad we see in our lives and the lives around us. When a loved one is going through cancer, God's character does not change. He still loves that person, He still continues to be faithful to her, even if it's not how we think it should look.

Father, humble our hearts. Help us to come to you in humility and to fully surrender to Your will. Instill Your goodness in our hearts and help us to trust Your ways, Your timing, and Your character. Open our eyes to the big picture and help us to see what You are doing. Thank you for your Word and for the reminder that Your heart is good, that You can be trusted and that You love us! In Jesus' name, Amen.

Reflection, Notes or Prayer

Day 3

"Your kingdom come, Your will be done, on earth as it is in heaven." – Matthew 6:10

PRAYING GOD'S WILL DURING HARDSHIP

God HIMSELF is always loving and good. God's WILL is always to glorify Himself and sometimes He glorifies Himself through our trials and hardships. God does not put us through trials and hardships deliberately, but He ALLOWS them, like when God ALLOWED Satan access in Job's life (Job 1:6-12).

Read Job 1:6-12 and record what God says to Satan to allow him access to Job:

_____

_____

At first glance (and maybe many more glances!) it's startling to read that God gave Satan access to Job, when God Himself said in verse 8, "Have you considered my servant Job? There is no one on earth like him; he is blameless and upright, a man who fears God and shuns evil." Whoa!! What in the world was God thinking?! Job continues to suffer and suffer and have hardship after hardship until chapter 38 when God finally speaks. God doesn't answer any of the questions that Job had been asking Him, but He proceeds to tell Job who HE is.

Read chapters 38-41 in Job.

After God reminds Job who He is, Job is almost speechless and I imagine in complete awe of God. Job responds to God in chapter 42 saying:

> *"I know that You can do all things; no purpose of Yours can be thwarted. You asked, 'Who is this that obscures My plans without knowledge?' Surely I spoke of things I did not understand, things too wonderful for me to know"* (2-3).

> Job continues, *"My ears had heard of You [God] but now my eyes have seen You. Therefore I despise myself and repent in dust and ashes"* (5-6).

Job admitted that before all of this happened, he had not really known God ("my ears had heard of You"), but "now my eyes have seen you". God used all of Job's hardship to open up his eyes to the majesty of God. Job was not the same person after his hardship. He had a newer, deeper reverence for God. Romans 8:28 says, "And we know that in all things, God works for the good of those who love Him." In God's great love for us, He allows us to go through trials for a greater purpose and we can trust that the greater purpose is always good.

Sin, the fact that we live in a broken world (with free will), and the fact that we have an enemy that wants to "kill, steal and destroy" is the ultimate cause of our trials and hardships. God will use the trials and hardships in our lives to bring us back to Himself and build a closer relationship with Him as we lean on Him through tough times.

God also uses trials and hardships to refine us. I can't tell you how many times I've gone through some really hard things, and if given the choice to do it over again, I would still choose the hard times. Hard times can teach us things that we wouldn't have otherwise known. They force us to dig deeper into God and into His Word. Hard times can spotlight things about ourselves that have held us back or they can reveal some wrong thinking. Many times, God heals us spiritually as we walk through our greatest fears and we come out stronger on the other side.

When we are praying for God's will to be done, it's so important that we look at our trials through a heavenly perspective. We often look at our trials through our circumstances: how we feel, how a situation is affecting us and those around us, how it affects our pocketbook, our comfort, and our security. But the challenge here is to look at our trials from God's perspective or a heavenly perspective. What is God doing on His throne that is affecting my world and why is He allowing it to happen? We know that He is 100% good and that there is NO evil in Him. There is no sin or darkness or false motive or manipulation in God so we can trust that whatever He is allowing us to go through, He is doing SOMETHING. That "something" is what we can keep our eyes fixed upon instead of keeping our eyes fixed on our circumstances.

Here are two Scriptures that are so dear to my heart. They are a reminder for me always to be looking at my life through a heavenly perspective:

Isaiah 55:8-9 *"For My thoughts are not your thoughts, neither are your ways My ways," declares the Lord. "As the heavens are higher than the earth, so are My ways higher than your ways and My thoughts than your thoughts."*

Colossians 3:2 *Set your mind on the things above, not on earthly things.*

Knowing that God's goodness is demonstrated even through our trials and hardships helps us to trust God's will over our own will even when His will doesn't look so great. True freedom comes when we are able to completely release control of our lives to the Creator of the Universe. We come to God boldly with our prayers, knowing that ultimately His will will be done!

Father, as hard as it is, we thank You for the trials and hardships in our lives. We thank You that You will use all the hardships in our lives for YOUR good. We thank You that we can trust You and that You are in complete control! In Jesus' name, Amen.

Reflection, Notes or Prayer

Day 4

"Your kingdom come, Your will be done, on earth as it is in heaven." – Matthew 6:10

PRAYING FOR OTHERS

Oh my goodness, my very favorite subject in the whole, wide world: praying for people (in person)! Now, don't get me wrong. You might remember from my first video that I would get sick to my stomach any time I THOUGHT I would have to pray in front of people. It has been a very uncomfortable journey from that point, but God has been with me the entire way. I can't tell you how many times He asked me to pray for people in the most awkward scenarios. God knows that I always *try* to conform my heart to a "Yes, Lord" posture, so He tends to take full advantage of that. It's saying "yes" to being uncomfortable that moves you into a new intimacy with God. Praying for other people in person has forced me to trust God in ways that I wouldn't have had to trust Him otherwise.

I have to be honest; I'm not a big, sit-in-the-corner-of-my-room-and-pray-for-other-people kind of girl. I do pray for others during my personal prayer time, but what I really love is praying for people in person. On one particular occasion, I was walking the mall with a friend. (Yes, for exercise. We live in Wisconsin and the winters can be quite brutal.) God asked me to pray for a man sitting on a bench in the mall. I was at a loss about what God wanted me to pray and as clear as a bell I heard God say, "I just want him to feel My touch through your prayer."

It was at that moment I was so convicted. Yes, the words we use in our prayers are important, but they're not as important as the act of obedience in praying for who God wants to touch. God uses us as the vehicle to affect people through prayer, but God is the one doing all of the work and the heavy lifting. He is the one who touches people through whatever words are spoken. He can enhance the simplest words to accomplish something profound. So many times we can get caught in the trap of making prayer all about us. How did the prayer sound? Was it moving? Was it powerful? Someone once told me that if you are worried about how your prayers sound, you are not praying to God, you are praying to yourself. Such a great meter to check ourselves!

God wants us to pray for people in person so they can feel God's touch.

Prayer is powerful and it works! It is an amazing way to share the love of Jesus and allow people who may not even believe that God exists to be touched by Him. How many times do you see someone struggling with some kind of hardship or some kind of trial? Jesus is the answer to all our problems and I truly believe that asking Him into our hardships and trials is half the battle. We forget to invite God into our circumstances. We are either so conditioned to take care of ourselves or we've been so disappointed in God that we don't bother inviting Him in because we don't think He's capable or we think that He doesn't want to help. Or that we are unworthy of His help. Well, I am here to say that those are ALL lies! God *wants* to help you, but more than that, He wants to be invited into all situations.

So we've determined that we are going to pray for people. Now how do we do it?

First of all, just pray. Just talk to God. Just ask God. You've got to start there. Once you've got that down, one of the most powerful things that you can do is start using Scripture in your prayers. Someone once said to me that when you pray God's Scripture back to Him through prayer, it's like you are speaking His language back to Him! What a great analogy to help us understand why there is so much power when praying Scripture over each other.

Prayer is a powerful tool that God gives us. The Word of God (Scripture) is a powerful tool that God gives us. When you put the two together, it makes double the impact!

There are many available books containing scripted prayers loaded with Scripture that we can be praying over people. These prayers are powerful and can teach us how to use Scripture in our own prayers. After praying through scripted prayers for a period of time, using Scripture in your prayers for others will become second nature. A couple of my favorite books containing these prayers are:

- *Prayers That Avail Much:25th Anniversary Edition* by Germaine Copeland [5]
- *The Power of a Praying...* series of books by Stormie Omartian[6] which focus on praying within our various roles (parent, wife, grandparent) and for various people (young children, adult children). Each book is broken into chapters containing a powerful prayer based on Scripture and listing all of the Scripture references.

The best part of using these books' examples of how to incorporate Scripture when praying for others is that we are reminded that God is the one who is going to fix whatever is broken. Many of us are naturally "fixers" or "doers" and we get ourselves into trouble when we rely on our own ability or knowledge to get the job done. When we invite Scripture into our prayers, it reminds us that God is the one who is going to do what needs to be done!

When praying for people, we must be confident that God is going to hear our prayer and that He's going to respond to our prayer. His response may not always be what we want, but we know that we can trust Him.

Please write out 1 John 5:14-15:

_____

_____

_____

Lastly, when praying for others, we want to invite the Holy Spirit to be our guide. We talked about this at length in Video 2, but I just wanted to quickly mention it again. *We* can come up with tons of things to pray, but unless we invite the Holy Spirit to speak through our prayers, our prayers will be powerless. We need to invite the power of the Holy Spirit to guide us when we pray.

In summary, when we are praying for others:

1. Come to Jesus with a <u>humble</u> and <u>surrendered</u> heart.
2. Invite God's will to be done.
3. Invite God's presence into their lives.
4. Ask boldly and confidently for what they need (using Scripture).
5. Invite the Holy Spirit to guide your prayers.

Close your eyes right now and ask God who needs to be prayed for. Pray for each one right now.

_____

_____

_____

_____

_____

_____

_____

_____

Father, thank You for teaching us how to pray for others. Thank You for showing us that You want to use us to bring Your perfect will to earth as it is in heaven. Thank You that You call us to pray when You want to change the natural course of events. Thank You that our prayers are heard and necessary. Thank You for allowing us to stand in the gap. We will answer Your call to pray! Please give me the boldness and courage I need to say "yes" to You when You prompt me to pray. In Jesus' name, Amen.

Reflection, Notes or Prayer

_____

_____

_____

Week Three

Give us today our daily bread.

Look Inward!

Video Three

(To watch *Video Three*, go to angelaackley.com)

Watch Video Three and use this space to take notes. You may want to jot down any Scriptures that speak to you or any comments or stories that you don't want to forget!

_____

_____

_____

_____

_____

_____

_____

_____

_____

_____

_____

_____

_____

_____

_____

_____

_____

_____

T his week we will be looking **inward** and will focus on praying for ourselves.

Day 1

"Give us today our daily bread." – Matthew 6:11

JESUS, OUR DAILY BREAD

Give us today our daily bread. I love this reminder that we need to look to God to be fed every day.

In Exodus 16 in the Old Testament, we learn that God provided physical food—manna, a type of bread—for the Israelites *every* day.

> *When the (morning) dew was gone, thin flakes like frost on the ground appeared on the desert floor. When the Israelites saw it, they said to each other, "What is it?" For they did not know what it was. Moses said to them, "It is the bread the Lord has given you to eat."* (14-15)

Moses then instructed them to only take as much as they needed.

> *However, some of them paid no attention to Moses; they kept part of it until morning, but it was full of maggots and began to smell.* (20)

This story makes me think of those times I've gone to my favorite restaurant to order my favorite meal. The meal comes out fresh and hot and delicious. It's so good that you don't want it to be over and you decide to take half of it home. The next day you're looking so forward to eating that other half! You take the first bite and are bitterly disappointed: the fries are soggy, the bread is stale, and everything else just tastes like cardboard. Ever had that happen?!? God is not the God of leftovers. **He wants to give us something new and fresh *every* day.**

It's easy to look at this passage—*Give us today our daily bread*—and assume that God wants to provide for us physically every day. But God also wants to provide for us spiritually. Jesus refers to Himself as the "bread of life." John 6:35 says, "Then Jesus declared, 'I am the bread of life. Whoever comes to Me will never go hungry, and whoever believes in Me will never be thirsty.'" Whoa! How cool is that! If we come to Jesus every day, we will never go hungry and if we believe in Him, we will never be thirsty. Don't you just want to stop right now and throw up a prayer of thanks to our Heavenly Father?!? Don't delay—do it right now!

We can easily understand how God wants to feed us physically, but what exactly does it mean to be fed *spiritually*? God feeds us spiritually through **prayer** and by **reading Scripture**. (From here on, we will assume any mention of "God's Word" or "reading the Bible" all means reading Scripture.) As we ask Him to feed us spiritually, we need to ask Him to feed us as three parts: our body, our soul, and our spirit. Genesis 1:27 reminds us that "God created mankind in His own image." God is of three parts (Father, Son, and Holy Spirit) just like we are of three parts (body, soul, and spirit).

Over the next three days we are going to explore how God wants to spiritually feed our body, soul, and spirit.

Father, I thank You that You are the Bread of Life and that You feed us something new and fresh every day. I thank You that You feed us physically and that You feed us spiritually. Open our eyes in the next few days as to what it means to be fed spiritually by You. Thank You for being our provider. In Jesus' name, Amen.

Reflection, Notes or Prayer

Day 2

"Give us today our daily bread." – Matthew 6:11

JESUS FEEDS OUR BODY

Today, we are going to start with asking Jesus to feed our BODY.

I don't know about you, but I have struggled with body image issues and eating issues my whole life, so the thought of asking Jesus to feed my body actually gives me peace. The thought of being able to turn my body over to Him and not have to strive gives me relief.

Just like so many things in life, Jesus asks us to lay certain things down before we can pick them back up again. Our bodies are no different. We need to lay our bodies down to our Creator so that He can fill them up. Have you ever stopped to think about handing your body over to Jesus? Have you ever dedicated your body to His work and His purposes? After all, God created us for His purposes. It's time to start living that out!

> *For we are God's handiwork, created in Christ Jesus* **to do good works** *, which God prepared in advance for us to do.* (Ephesians 2:10, emphasis mine)

Honestly, it was after I first dedicated my body to Jesus and to His good works that many of my struggles with my body started to come to light. It was definitely a turning point in my life and quite frankly, a whole new way to view my body. The passage in 1 Corinthians 6:19 really helps us see how God wants us to view our body: "Do you not know that your bodies are temples of the Holy Spirit, who is in you, whom you have received from God? You are not your own."

Did you catch the last sentence of that passage? Write out the last sentence:

_____

_____

We are not our own. Our bodies are the temples of His Holy Spirit. Let's make it official. (This dedication is going to take at least a half hour, so if you don't have time to do it right now, grab your phone and schedule a half-hour slot in the next week to do so. It's important, so please don't forget!)

Are you ready? Lie down on your back and close your eyes. **Dedicate each specific part of your body to Jesus** so that He can use your body for His purposes. I've made a list to help you. It may seem funny to dedicate some of the body parts that I've listed to Jesus, but we want to give Him our WHOLE body so that He has full access to make sure that everything is functioning as it should be. Once you finish dedicating your body, spend some time thanking God for your body! Here is the list:

Brain	Breasts	Bowels
Ears	Lungs	Bladder
Eyes	Airways	Liver
Nose	Circulatory system	"Private" Parts
Mouth	Lymphatic system	Legs
Voice	Nervous system	Knees
Arms	Skeletal system	Ankles
Hands	Stomach	Feet
Heart	Kidneys	

Father, thank You for this gift, this body that You have given me. Thank You that our bodies are homes for the Holy Spirit. What an honor that You would use our bodies to live in. Help us to view our bodies the way You view them. Help us to see our bodies through Your eyes. Help us to love and take care of our bodies like they are the gift they were intended to be. In Jesus' name, Amen.

Reflection, Notes or Prayer

_____

_____

_____

Day 3

"Give us today our daily bread." – Matthew 6:11

JESUS FEEDS OUR SOUL

Good news: Jesus feeds our soul! But wait—what even is our soul? Our soul is defined as our will, our mind, and our emotions. It's the part of us that carries our personality and human feelings. It's the part of us, quite frankly, that we allow to rule over us most of the time.

Yes, I'm sorry to say that most of us put ourselves at the center of our universe. We want *our* will, we use *our own* reason to figure things out and many times we are led by *our* emotions... and that is precisely why we need Jesus to "feed our soul." We want to be led by the Father, Son, and Holy Spirit, not OUR own will, mind, or emotions.

- We all have hopes, dreams, expectations (our **WILL**).
- We all have knowledge and we reason through situations (our **MIND**).
- We all have differences in how we *feel* about certain topics, situations, or circumstances (our **EMOTIONS**).

I want to make it very clear that our soul (will, mind, and emotions) can mislead us. It's really important here to catch the fact that our feelings and emotions are not the indicator of truth. If left to ourselves, we start to believe untruths and lies. We start to use reason to get our answers and let our emotions drive how we act or behave. Let's be honest, I think all of us can admit that if we allowed our emotions to be our truth to lead and direct our lives when dealing with hormones, our lives would be an absolute mess!! Our soul needs to be fed daily by Jesus so that HE is in control of our will, our mind, and our emotions.

Will

Jesus, feed our will. Let's take a look at our will. How many of us would reach the destiny God has for our lives if we followed our own will? Do you think that the will that God has for your life looks exactly like the will you have for your life? I don't know about you, but up until this point in my life, the will that I have had for my life has looked nothing like the will that God is revealing to me. And His is WAY better! The longer I walk with God, the more I realize that His ways are mind-blowing. His ways are nothing I could ever come up with. Our minds are so much simpler than His and the way He does things is so amazing to watch. I find myself reflecting on my past and am continually bewildered how He has gone about taking me where I am today. Things that I thought were a waste or meaningless have turned out to be useful and have helped prepare me for what is to come.

For example, right out of high school I attended college. I graduated with a business degree and only ended up working for five years before I stayed home to raise my children. I didn't like the business world and never had any plans to return. What a waste of time, right? Little did I know that years later God would place on my heart to start a Christ-based homeless shelter for single moms and their children. God placed the need in my heart and a group of us prayerfully sought His will until we had an 11-room shelter that holds 40 homeless women and their children. My business degree helped us tremendously in starting the shelter and God knew all those years ago that what seemed a waste to me was going to be used for His purposes.

When we ask Jesus to feed our souls, we are asking Him to align His will with our will. We are asking Him to impart His will for our lives into our hearts so that we desire and move into the direction He has for our lives.

Father, I am beyond grateful that You have a will for my life. I thank You that I don't have to make Your will happen, but that You will reveal it to me in Your timing. Thank You that Your plans for me are good, that they are plans to prosper me and not to harm me, to give me a hope and a future. Jesus, feed my will. In Jesus' name, Amen.

Mind

Jesus, feed our mind. Part of our souls are made up of our mind and our thoughts. Over our lifetime, we gain a lot of knowledge. We take that knowledge and we use it to reason and make good decisions. We gather information and we seek knowledge from others. We read books, we do our research. We then base our decisions and life choices on the deductive reasoning from these sources. This is how we are taught in school and this is the way the world teaches us. These are great tools in decision-making and for gaining direction, but as Christians, we need to invite another piece to this formula. We need to ask Jesus to feed our minds.

Proverbs 3: 5-6 (NLT) says, "Trust in the Lord with all your heart, **do not depend on your own understanding**. Seek His will in all you do and He will show you what path to take (emphasis mine).

So many times we reason and try to figure things out on our own without inviting God in. I've found in my own life that what seems to make the most sense and what seems to be the right way is not God's way at all. I have a dear friend who coined a phrase that I use quite often: "God does weird things." Very rarely can we try and figure out what He's doing or what His plans are. His ways and plans seem weird or wrong or complicated, but in hindsight, they always make sense. Just like it says in the Romans 8:28 (NLT) verse I've quoted in previous weeks, "… we know that God causes everything to work together for the good of those who love God and are called according to His purpose for them." God wants to be invited to feed every area of your life, including your mind.

Not only do our minds contain knowledge, but in our minds we also learn how to deal with certain emotions and in the process accumulate hurts and wounds. Our minds are powerful in moving us forward, but our minds can also trick us. Have you heard of the term "battlefield of the mind?" We have three voices constantly talking to us. We talk to ourselves, God talks to us (through the Holy Spirit), and the enemy (Satan) talks to us. As we spend more and more time with God, we begin to be able to discern which voice we are hearing. When we ask Jesus to feed our thoughts, we are asking Him to turn up His voice so that we know it's Him talking to us.

Father, I thank You that You are the wisest in the whole universe. Thank You that You tell us not to depend on our own understanding, but that we need to seek Your will in all we do and You will tell us what path to take. There is no amount of knowledge or studying that can take the place of inviting You into our minds to think the way YOU want us to think! Jesus, fill my mind. In Jesus' name, Amen.

Emotions

Jesus, feed our emotions. Our emotions can really get the best of us if we let them. If we are not careful, we allow our emotions to make decisions for us. If we are stressed out, anxious, offended, fearful, or angry, chances are that we are not going to be able to say the right thing or act the right way. We must learn to recognize that when we are emotional or we are feeling a certain way, it's a sign we need to call on Jesus to feed our emotions so they don't lead us astray.

I don't know about you, but sometimes when I know that I am being totally unreasonable, I just don't care and I can't seem to stop. It seems to happen to me when I'm tired, overly hungry, feeling sorry for myself, or dealing with disappointment. I *know* that what is coming out of my mouth is wrong, but in some very twisted way, it feels good. When we get to that place, it's our cue to call on Jesus to feed our emotions. We need to invite Him in so that we see our situation clearly without our emotions muddling things.

When was the last time you had an emotional moment? Where you knew you were acting unjustly, but you just didn't care or you didn't know how to get out of it? Brand that moment in your memory so the next time that it happens, you will remember to pray and ask Jesus to feed your emotions.

Write your moment here:

_____

_____

_____

We need to surrender our emotions to the God of the Universe so that He can feed us. I love how Psalm 139:24 (NLT) teaches us how to do that. It says, "Point out anything in me that offends you, and lead me along the path of everlasting life." Let Him show you how you are acting and then let Him show you how to fix it!

Father, thank You that You are bigger than my emotions. Thank You that You see everything through the eyes of truth. You are not hindered by anxiety, fear, anger, offense, or any other emotion. Help me to see my situation through Your eyes. Feed my emotions so that they would be healthy and would not hinder me in the way I see or act. Point out anything in me that offends You, and lead me along the path of everlasting life. Jesus, fill my emotions. In Jesus' name, Amen.

Reflection, Notes or Prayer

_____

_____

_____

_____

_____

_____

_____

_____

_____

_____

_____

_____

_____

_____

Day 4

"Give us today our daily bread." – Matthew 6:11

JESUS FEEDS OUR SPIRIT

We all have a human spirit. It's that part of us that is always yearning for connection with God. It's the hole we feel in our gut before we invite in the Holy Spirit. If you invited the Holy Spirit into your life at a young age, you may not know what I'm talking about because you haven't known any difference and that is great! But for the rest of us, we have walked a part of our life without knowing God and we were always trying to fill that hole with something: shopping, money, success, cars, houses, sex, drugs, alcohol, or any other aspiration that when reached leaves us empty and unfulfilled.

Think about it...do you know anyone like that? Anyone who is always searching for the next high? Or maybe that is you right now. Our human spirit is yearning for the Holy Spirit to enter into our human spirit. Without the Holy Spirit taking up residence in our human spirit, we will never be complete. We will walk around empty, always feeling like we are missing something. But Jesus is the good news! When we invite Jesus to be our Lord and Savior and ask Him to forgive us of our sins, the Holy Spirit enters us and we are filled.

It's always so important to confirm any teaching with the Word of God, so please look up Romans 8:16 and write it below:

_____

_____

I'm going to stop right here for a quick minute. If you have never asked Jesus to be your Lord and Savior, I would invite you to do that right now. It's so easy; all you have to do is pray this simple prayer out loud right now.

Jesus, I invite You into my heart to be my Lord and my Savior. I believe that You died and were raised again for my sins. Please forgive me of all my sins. Thank You for giving me the gift of the Holy Spirit. Amen!

If you just prayed that prayer for the first time, I want to personally welcome you into the family of God! God now lives in you through the Holy Spirit and He will NEVER leave you! He is the voice of God that counsels you, guides you, comforts you, and so much more.

A couple of years ago, my father and my brother passed away eight days apart. Shortly after their passing, in my prayer time I was asking the Lord to show me how we get to heaven. He showed me that because our human spirit and the Holy Spirit become merged together when we invite Jesus to be our Lord and Savior, when our human bodies pass away, the Holy Spirit goes back to heaven and takes *our* spirit with Him! Isn't that cool?! We get a free plane ride with the Holy Spirit back to heaven where our spirit lives in eternity.

Once again, let's confirm what the Lord showed me with this passage from Scripture. Please look up and write out 2 Corinthians 1:22 (NIV translation is best here):

So now that we know that we *have* a human spirit and that the Holy Spirit has taken residence in our spirit, we need to feed our spirit. How do we do that? Well, remember that we define our human spirit as the part of us that is always yearning for connection with God. In order to feed our spirit, we need to do those things that help us connect to God. We need to read His Word (the Bible). We need to sit in His presence and praise Him. We need to spend *more* time with Him. We need to be still and listen to Him (*Be still and know that I am God*—Psalm 46:10). We need to pray.

We need to ask Jesus to feed our spirit through Scripture and through prayer, which includes praise, being still, and listening.

Jesus, thank You for the gift of the Holy Spirit. Thank You that You are filling more and more of our human spirit. We want You to overcome us and we want to be full of the Holy Spirit. Help us to spend more time with You, to sit in Your presence and to hear Your voice. Give us a hunger and a thirst to read Your Word. Fill our spirits to overfilling.

Give us this day our daily bread and feed our entire being: our body, our soul, and our spirit.
In Jesus' name, Amen.

Reflection, Notes or Prayer

_____

_____

_____

_____

_____

_____

_____

_____

_____

_____

_____

_____

_____

_____

_____

_____

_____

_____

_____

_____

Week Four

And forgive us our debts, as we also have forgiven our debtors.

Confession

Video Four

(To watch Video Four, go to angelaackley.com)

Watch Video Four and use this space to take notes. You may want to jot down any Scriptures that speak to you or any comments or stories that you don't want to forget!

_____

_____

_____

_____

_____

_____

_____

_____

_____

_____

_____

_____

_____

_____

_____

_____

_____

_____

_____

Week Four

This week we will be looking at **confession** for the forgiveness of our sins.

Day 1

"And forgive us our debts, as we also have forgiven our debtors."– Matthew 6:12

WHAT'S THE BIG DEAL ABOUT CONFESSION?

When I first joined a Moms In Prayer group, we would come to the Confession part of our prayer time and I had no clue what I was supposed to be doing. (The Moms In Prayer organization follows the ACTS method of prayer: Adoration, Confession, Thanksgiving, and Supplication.) We would start with "Adoration" (I call it "praising God" in this study) and then the prayer host would move us into "C", a time of silent confession. I would sit with my eyes closed during this Confession time and patiently wait until the silence was over and we moved into a time of Thanksgiving.

It may sound silly to you that I didn't know what to do during confession, but as a newer believer, I was never taught why or how I should confess. So if I was feeling this way, I'm sure there are one or two of you out there who could use some explanation as well!

To be honest, confession is one of the biggest deals in prayer. On days where I am short on prayer time, I get in at least my praise time and confession time. Those two are important because praise ushers us into the presence of God and confession releases us from any bondage or strongholds that our own sin (or our unforgiveness of others' sin) holds over us. I'll be going into more detail on this later, but basically confession allows for spiritual healing. Many people have never heard the term "spiritual healing" but we've all heard of physical healing. Like we learned last week, we are both physical and spiritual beings and we need to take care of each aspect. We know how physical healing works because we see it every day. Spiritual healing is a bit more complicated because we can't see it. We all experience spiritual hurts and wounds from our own sin and from unfavorable circumstances or trauma in our lives. Those hurts and wounds can stay with us, so God wants to heal us from their traumatic impact.

Our time of confession with the Lord entails prayer that requires us to listen to what the Lord is saying and requires us to ask the Lord questions. I'm sure many people simply say something like this during their confession time: "Lord, forgive me for my thoughts, my words, and my deeds." While this is a good start, the Lord really wants us to get to the nuts and bolts of what we need to confess. The more detail we give, the better the results will be. For example, simply saying, "Forgive me for being mean" is necessary, but not quite enough. You need to be specific about exactly what you did that was mean so that you're being honest with yourself and with God about exactly what you did.

So how does confession work? Here's how: when Jesus died on the cross, ALL the sins of the world fell on his shoulders. Every. Single. Sin. ALL of your sins, my sins, our spouses' sins, our children's sins, our parents' sins, our grandparents' sins, our great-grandparents' sins, our great-great-grandparents' sins, our ENTIRE family line's sins...EVERYBODY'S sins as well as sins that haven't even been committed yet! He paid the price for all sins.

Therefore, because of what Jesus did on the cross, He has the authority to forgive us of our sins. All we have to do is admit our sins to God and He will forgive us! Confession is *a formal statement admitting that one is guilty of a crime.*[7] Admitting our sins to our forgiving God FREES us from the penalty of our sin and also FREES us from the pain of the wrong that we have done in our lives and the pain others have done to us. Doesn't that sound wonderful?!

As we venture into this next week of homework, hold on as we dig deep and allow the Holy Spirit to reveal who we have wronged and what we need to ask forgiveness for, and who has wronged us and what we need to forgive others for! It's going to be a challenging week, but one that will change you from the inside out.

Much of the work of confession can simply be done between you and God, but I have found in my years of praying with people that James 5:16 is true. It says, "Confess your sins to each other and pray for each other so that you may be healed." Most times simply confessing to God will bring you freedom, but there are times where God will ask you to confess to God through prayer with another person. Since that may be the case for you, start praying that God would bring that safe person to you. It could be a friend or it could be a stranger (or even a counselor), but the key is to confess only to someone that you feel completely comfortable with.

There is FREEDOM in confession!!!

Before we end our time together today, please open your Bible to Psalm 51. David wrote this Psalm after he had committed adultery with Bathsheba. He not only committed adultery, but he also had Bathsheba's husband murdered. David teaches us in this Psalm how to come to the Father and admit our guilt and how to repent.

Please write out Psalm 51.

_____

_____

_____

_____

_____

_____
_____
_____
_____
_____
_____
_____
_____
_____
_____
_____
_____
_____
_____
_____
_____
_____
_____

Father, we need You this week more than ever. I pray a hedge of protection around each and every one of us. I pray that You would put Your finger on those hurts and wounds that You want to heal and that we would all experience great freedom through our confession time with You. Thank You, Jesus, for dying on the cross and conquering death so that we can be forgiven of our sins. You paid the price for us and for that we will be forever grateful! Please bring a safe person across our path to pray with as we seek freedom in Your name. We pray all these things in Your holy name, Jesus. Amen.

Reflection, Notes or Prayer

_____
_____
_____

DAY 1

Day 2

"And forgive us our debts, as we also have for-given our debtors."– Matthew 6:12

ASKING GOD FOR FORGIVENESS

Let's open our day together with re-reading Psalm 51.

We need to set aside time every day for confession. I know that we all have crazy schedules and I never want to come across as legalistic or make you feel guilty for not praying enough. But we should be aware that our sins can build up like a stinky pile of laundry. (Trust me on the stinky-pile-of-laundry thing: our washing machine just got fixed after being broken for seven weeks with three teenage boys in the house! Have mercy!) Anyway, the longer we wait to wash the laundry (i.e., confess), the more the stinky clothes (sins) pile up and the harder we have to work to get them clean. Are you seeing the analogy here?

If confession isn't something that you've done for a while (or ever done), you are going to need to spend more time up front, but in the long run when you are doing it every day, it will be a breeze! Now hear me clearly: I'm not judging you. Remember, I became a Christian in my early 20's and it was about 10 more years before I actually knew the importance of confession, so I had a whole lot of dirty laundry to clean!

The beauty of what Jesus did for us on the cross is seen in the following verses. This is SUCH exciting news for us and I want you to let this sink in deep.

Look up and write the following verses:

Hebrews 8:12

_____

_____

Isaiah 43:25

_____

_____

When we ask for forgiveness, He will remember our sins no more AND He will never think of them again! How can it be that easy?!? It *is* that easy. The hard part for some of us is accepting that, but we will talk about that on Day 4.

So why do we need to confess our sins? Here's the clincher: sin separates us from God. I like to explain it this way. Picture your heart. Now picture God in heaven shining His light directly to your heart. Now picture your heart with black smudges all over it (representing sin). The black smudges are areas in your heart that God does not have access to. When we have sin in our lives, that sin blocks out God's light and denies Him access to those areas. I want every piece of my heart to have full access to God's light. When God isn't allowed access, we struggle with things on our own and we are left without all that God has to offer us.

Today I want you to spend some time with God. Ask Him what you need to ask forgiveness for. When we ask this question, many times we are surprised by the answer. He may bring very recent things to mind or He may remind you of something from when you were a child. It's very important to remember that when God brings these things to mind, it's to heal you, not to torture you with your past! Be careful not to dwell on whatever He brings to mind. Ask forgiveness and then move on. Remember that He says in Hebrews 8:12 that "he remembers your sins no more" once you've asked for forgiveness. If the issues don't seem to be going away, you may need to call on that safe friend that I talked about on Day 1 of this week (or a Christian counselor) and the two of you can pray through asking for forgiveness.

Be aware that when you start those first couple loads of laundry after not having done it for 30 years, it seems that more laundry keeps coming. There will be times when the Lord will bring to mind past sin even when you aren't praying about it. Once again, God is not condemning you about your past. He's just bringing it to mind so that you can confess it and move on! The Lord is ready to clean your dirty laundry. Embrace it!

Ask the Lord to reveal any past mistakes or sin that you need to confess. Remember to get detailed! Write them down and then confess them to God.

_____

_____

_____

_____

There is a second piece to this process. In addition to past mistakes and sin, we also believe lies. Where do these lies come from, you might ask? You may not realize it, but we are talking to ourselves all day long...and most of the time, not with positive stuff. We hear lies about ourselves all the time—*You're too fat... You're stupid... You're worthless... You're hopeless... You're a terrible mother... You're not good enough for your wife*—and sometimes, we believe them. Once we believe a lie, we begin to act and think like it's truth. Our lens of reality gets distorted and we become in bondage to the lie that we have believed.

In our confession time, it's very important that we ask God to bring to mind any lies that we've believed. When He brings those to mind, remember: it's not to condemn us but to free us. We simply ask forgiveness for believing that lie.

It goes something like this:

God, please forgive me for believing the lie that I am a terrible mother. I renounce that lie in Jesus' name and I ask You to sever any ties to that lie. What is the truth?

And then wait to hear the truth that God wants to speak to your heart.

Ask the Lord to reveal any lies that you have been believing. Remember to get detailed! Write them down and then confess them to God using the prayer above.

_____

_____

_____

_____

Father, I thank You that when I confess my sins, when I confess my guilt, You remember my sins no more. Thank You, Jesus, for what You did on the cross and thank You for bringing up dirty old laundry so it can finally get cleaned. Thank You for forgiving me. In Jesus' name, Amen.

Reflection, Notes or Prayer

_____

_____

_____

_____

_____

_____

_____

_____

_____

_____

_____

_____

_____

_____

_____

_____

_____

_____

_____

Day 3

"And forgive us our debts, as we also have forgiven our debtors."– Matthew 6:12

FORGIVING OTHERS AND OURSELVES

On Day 1 we talked about how God wants to give us spiritual healing of any hurts and wounds we bear from traumatic experiences in our lives.

What are some of the hurts and wounds that you would like the Lord to heal?

_____

_____

When you think of those hurts and wounds, does anyone come to mind that you may need to forgive?

_____

_____

Forgiveness is a complicated subject. I want to start off by saying that sometimes we refuse to forgive someone because what they did to us was wrong and we want them to pay for what they did. We think that if we forgive them, their actions are affirmed. THAT IS NOT TRUE! When we forgive someone, it does not mean what they did to us was OK and it doesn't let them off the hook. When we forgive, it simply releases *us* from the sin of holding onto unforgiveness.

As we talked about on Day 2, sin separates us from God. Holding onto unforgiveness is a sin and it separates us from God. When we forgive, we are not letting people off the hook or giving the impression that what they did was OK. We are simply removing sin from our life.

Our job is not to make people pay for their sin or hold them accountable for their sin. That is God's job. Someday, each one of us will stand before the Lord and be held accountable for the sin in our lives. God's wrath over that sin is much more than we could ever impose against someone. That person's sin is between them and God. God *will* deal with them. Let God do the heavy lifting of justice. You just worry about yourself and getting yourself healthy.

So what does the Bible say about forgiving others? Look up and write out the following verses. This part is very important so please don't skip over it!

Matthew 6:14-15 (KEY)**

_____

_____

Matthew 18:21-22

_____

_____

Mark 11:25-26

_____

_____

Ephesians 4:32

_____

_____

Colossians 3:13

_____

_____

Scripture constantly reminds us that we need to forgive. When ideas or thoughts are repeated in Scripture, that should signal us that we need to pay attention. This is one of those ideas or thoughts that we need to take seriously. I'm going to explain why shortly, but for now, trust me!

Please re-read Matthew 6:14-15 and Mark 11:25-26. Both of these passages highlight that if we don't forgive, WE WON'T BE FORGIVEN! Go ahead and underline those words in both of the passages that you wrote down above.

We need to forgive not only to remove sin in our lives, but also so that we can be forgiven. We don't want to be stuck in a certain area in our life because we are being too stubborn to forgive.

Look up Matthew 7:3 and write it below:

_____

_____

Lord, help us to see *our own* sin instead of focusing on the sins of others!

So far we've covered that we need to forgive **to remove sin** (1) and **so that we can be forgiven** (2), but there is one more important reason. We also need to forgive **so that resentment, anger, and bitterness do not begin to grow** (3). Remember when I said that we have to take this topic seriously? The reason is that unforgiveness breeds resentment, anger, and bitterness, and the longer we hold onto our unforgiveness, the deeper the roots of resentment, anger, and bitterness will grow. Over time these roots grow into plants that choke out joy, peace, and contentment, and we are pulled further and further from our intimacy with God. Our unforgiveness continues to feed those roots and they continue to grow over time. If you are experiencing resentment, anger, or bitterness regularly, you are probably holding onto unforgiveness towards at least one person, maybe more.

Scripture makes it very clear that we need to ask for forgiveness and forgive others, but Scripture isn't so clear on needing to forgive ourselves, probably because we don't have the power to forgive ourselves. But I challenge you to think about the reason you would need to forgive yourself. It may not be what you think.

The reason we would need to forgive ourselves is because we don't believe that we have been forgiven. We are sinning in our *unbelief.* When we forgive ourselves, we are really admitting our unbelief that we have already been forgiven. On Day 1 of this week we looked at two verses in Scripture that told us that when we ask for forgiveness, <u>He will remember our sins no more</u> and <u>He will never think of them again</u>! When we beat ourselves up over the past mistakes that we've made or we beat ourselves up over how selfish we've been, we condemn ourselves over and over and over again. Romans 8:1 says, "there is now no condemnation for those who are in Christ Jesus." Please underline the words "no condemnation." **If we are in Christ and He is in us, we cannot condemn ourselves because He does not condemn us!**

I've prayed with lots of people through deliverance prayer (deliverance means "the action of being set free").[8] One of the most common things I have seen is that we need to forgive ourselves for our past mistakes, for hurting people, for our selfishness, for sinning against our bodies, and countless other things that we feel like we can't be forgiven for. <u>Confess the sin of unbelief</u>! Friends, God WANTS to heal you. We just need to know what His Word says and then we need to do it! I know that you are eager to dig in and start your forgiveness journey, but you'll have to wait for tomorrow. Let's ask God to prepare us for our heavy lifting tomorrow where we learn the tools and the method for forgiveness.

Father, I thank You for Your Word. When we dig into Your Word and begin to understand why You say what You do, we begin to experience You on a deeper level. Thank You for loving us so much that You have given us the best handbook and guide, the Bible. Thank You that You forgive us and remember our sins no more. Thank You that when we forgive others, You forgive us. Prepare our hearts to be set free as we dive deeper into releasing the sins of unforgiveness and unbelief. We are so grateful that we know You and that You are the only one who can offer us true freedom. We love You! In Jesus' name, Amen

Reflection, Notes or Prayer

Day 4

"And forgive us our debts, as we also have for-
given our debtors."– Matthew 6:12

HOW TO FORGIVE

Welcome back! So glad you are still here! Today is when things are going to start to get a little prickly, but please promise me that you will work today's lesson until the end. If you are squirming in your seat right now because you already know the list of people that you need to forgive, don't panic. We are going to walk through this together.

By now I hope that you are one hundred percent clear (and sure) that you need to forgive. <u>Please realize that forgiveness is a process</u>. Many times, forgiveness is not a one-shot deal. The longer unforgiveness has been around, the longer it takes to remove it, layer by layer. So many times, I pray with people and they say, "I thought I already forgave so-and-so!" My answer to that is you probably forgave them for certain things, but there are other things that need to be uncovered. I don't want to discourage you by saying that it's a process, but I don't want you to think that all unforgiveness is going to go away overnight either. It can—it sure can, and if that's how it happens for you, praise God!—but from what I've seen, it's usually a process.

Having said that, if bad memories or thoughts continue to resurface after you have forgiven (or asked for forgiveness), I urge you to dig deeper into exactly *what* you need to forgive them (or yourself) for. If you get to the point where you are stuck and nothing you do seems to work, you will probably need to contact that safe person to pray these things through (or maybe a pastor or Christian counselor). Remember that James 5:16 says that when we confess our sins to one another *then* we will be healed.

Let's get started!

Because Scripture clearly says that we will be forgiven if we forgive others, we want to start with forgiving others. I realize that the following exercises are going to take WAY longer than the time that you have set aside for your study today, so I am going to give you instruction and then you can choose when you are going to do it. I would suggest grabbing your calendar at this point and scheduling three (3) one-hour time slots in the next two weeks to get you started. If you are super ambitious and want to experience freedom as soon as possible, schedule them within a week. There is no formula. The point is just to do it and not forget about it! The process isn't always fun, but the FREEDOM that you experience afterwards is priceless. You are going to want to grab a pen and paper. Here we go!

Forgiving Others

1. Ask the Lord who you need to forgive. When you have that person in mind, ask the Lord what you need to forgive them for.
2. Make a list and write down each and every thing that you need to forgive them for.
3. After your list is complete, turn each one of those offenses into a heavy brick. Your heavy bricks represent the pain, the bitterness, the guilt, the fear, or anything else that has kept you in bondage. Now imagine carrying around those bricks in a giant backpack. Allow yourself to feel the weight.
4. Now dump out all your bricks. Every item on your list represents a brick, so grab each brick individually and say out loud, "I forgive _____ for _____." Then take that brick and put it back into the backpack. When you are all done, hand your backpack full of bricks over to God. Give Him all the weight that you have been carrying around.
5. Rip up your list and throw it away!
6. **Pray a prayer to bless this person**. Pray for their salvation, for their healing, for their peace, and that God would bless them (and anything else that comes to mind). When we pray for someone who has hurt us, our bitter feelings begin to change and we begin to have a new heart and compassion for that person. The beautiful part is that it is God who is giving you a new heart of compassion; it's not something we have to muster up on our own. God changes our heart toward that person through prayer. This is a big deal, so please don't skip this step!
7. Continue to ask the Lord if there is anyone else you need to forgive. Continue this process until nobody else comes to mind.

Asking for Forgiveness

1. Ask the Lord how you have sinned against Him. *What do I need forgiveness for?*
2. Make a list and write down each and every thing that you need forgiveness for.
3. Read down your list and say out loud, "Please forgive me for _____."
4. Ask the Lord if there is anyone with whom you need to meet face-to-face to apologize and ask for forgiveness.
5. Write those people down on a separate sheet of paper.
6. Rip up your list of forgiveness from #2 and throw it away!
7. Pray and thank God for forgiving you and thank Jesus for dying for your sins.

If, in steps #4 and #5 above, the Lord brought someone (or multiple people) to mind with whom you need to meet face-to-face to apologize and ask them to forgive you, stop right here. Before you do this, you need to be certain that *God* is the one prompting this meeting. Sometimes our own will or plagued conscience might bring people to mind and we want to be entirely sure that it is God prompting this meeting. So before you act, please take your time and continue to ask God to confirm that He has indeed prompted the face-to-face meeting.

Once you feel peace about the face-to-face meeting and God has confirmed that He is asking you to schedule the meeting, go ahead and make the contact.

Forgiving Ourselves

1. Ask the Lord what you need to forgive yourself for.
2. Make a list and write down each and every thing that you need to forgive yourself for.
3. Before you begin, ask the Lord to forgive you of any unbelief you have and to replace it with assurance that He has already paid the price for your sins. Thank Jesus for paying that price.
4. Read down your list and say out loud, "I forgive myself for _____".
5. Rip up your list and throw it away!
6. Ask God to bless you and cover you with His Spirit.

Forgiveness for Believing Lies

1. Ask God what lies you have been believing.

2. Write them down.
3. One at a time, ask God to forgive the lie, renounce the lie and sever any ties to the lie.

Confession (admitting guilt and then asking for forgiveness) is a great big deal in receiving spiritual freedom. When we go through the hard work of cleaning up our old dirty laundry, our hurts and wounds no longer have control over us and we are left with peace and contentment. Doesn't that sound good? That's why I love Jesus so much! It's what He did for us so that we can be free! Stop carrying around that backpack of bricks. Unload what Jesus already paid the price for. "So, if the Son sets you free, you will be free indeed" (John 8:36)!

Lastly, remember a couple of weeks ago when we dedicated our bodies to Jesus? I hope that you did that because now we need to move on to Step 2 of that process. At some point (it would be wise to schedule it in your calendar right now), we need to go through that same list and ask God to forgive us for using any part of our body to sin against Him. For example, "Forgive me, God, for using my eyes to look at things that I shouldn't have been looking at." Then list out all the specific ways you sinned using your eyes. Or "Forgive me, God, for using my hands to do things that sinned against you" and then list out all of the specific ways you sinned against Him using your hands.

This last exercise will give you tremendous freedom! Go back to Week 2 and pray through the "body parts" list!

Father, thank You for teaching us about Your forgiveness. You forgave us first so that we could forgive others. We pray that You would set us free. Free from anger, resentment, and bitterness. Free from self-condemnation. Free from the lies that we've been believing. Free from the sin that entangles us. Free from the way we've used our bodies to sin. Thank You for paying the price, Jesus, so that we can be free!!! In Your name, Amen.

Reflection, Notes or Prayer

Week Five

And lead us not into temptation, but deliver us from the evil one.

Praying Protection

Video Five

(To watch *Video Five*, go to angelaackley.com)

Watch Video Five and use this space to take notes. You may want to jot down any Scriptures that speak to you or any comments or stories that you don't want to forget!

_____

_____

_____

_____

_____

_____

_____

_____

_____

_____

_____

_____

_____

_____

_____

_____

_____

_____

Week Five

This week we will be looking at praying for *protection*.

Day 1

"And lead us not into temptation, but deliver us from the evil one." – Matthew 6:13

WHO IS SATAN ANYWAY?

This week we are tackling the topic of spiritual warfare. Spiritual warfare is defined as "fighting against the work of evil forces based on the biblical belief in evil spirits, or demons, that are said to intervene in human affairs in various ways."[9]

At this point you may either be quaking in your boots or you are so excited (like me) that you can hardly stand it. Let me just say that it is crucial to have a good understanding of this subject. Jesus has been teaching us how to pray through the Lord's Prayer and I believe He had a good reason for saving temptation and evil until the end of the prayer. Up to this point, we have learned about praising God, praying for others, praying for ourselves, and confession. Only when we have a good understanding of those things can we dive into the deeper, more mature topic of spiritual warfare. I believe that ALL people should have a basic knowledge of spiritual warfare because whether we like to admit it or not, there is an unseen spiritual world and the war that is raging there affects us more than we understand.

We have a spiritual enemy and his name is Satan. John 10:10 describes this enemy. It says, "The thief comes only to **steal**, **kill** and **destroy**; I (Jesus) have come that they may have life, and have it to the full." We have a spiritual enemy that wants to steal, kill and destroy, but Jesus has come to rescue us from this enemy!!!

When we find ourselves in a war yet are completely unaware of our enemy, we are left powerless. If you look back at the history of war, you will notice that commanders spent considerable time studying their adversary. We need to do the same thing. So let's get started!

I'm using an excerpt from the book *Systematic Theology*[10] to give you a background of where the spiritual battle and evil began:

> *When God created the world, he "saw everything that he had made, and behold, it was very good" (Gen. 1:31). This means that even the angelic world that God had created did not have evil angels or demons in it at that time. But by the time of Genesis 3, we find that Satan, in the form of a serpent, was tempting Eve to sin (Gen. 3:1-5). Therefore, sometime between the events of Genesis 1:31 and Genesis 3:1, there must have been a rebellion in the angelic world and many angels turning against God and becoming evil.*

> *The New Testament speaks of this in two places. Peter tells us, "God did not spare the angels when they sinned, but cast them into hell and committed them to pits of nether gloom to be kept until the judgment" (2 Peter 2:4). Jude also says that "the angels that did not keep their own position but left their proper dwelling have been kept by him in eternal chains in the nether gloom until the judgment of the great day" (Jude 6). Once again the emphasis is on the fact that they are removed from the glory of God's presence and their activity is restricted, but the text does not imply either that the influence of demons has been removed from the world or that some*

demons are kept in a place of punishment apart from the world while others are able to influence it. Rather, both 2 Peter and Jude tell us that some angels rebelled against God and became hostile opponents to his Word. Their sin seems to have been pride, a refusal to accept their assigned place, for they "did not keep their own position but left their proper dwelling (Jude 6)."[11]

This text is saying that God originally created the world without evil. At some point between Genesis 1:31 and Genesis 3, some kind of angelic rebellion happened and many angels turned against God and became evil, committing the sin of pride.[12]

Isaiah 14:12-15 further describes this pride and rebellion. Let's read it together:

How you have fallen from heaven, morning star, son of the dawn! You have been cast down to the earth, you who once laid low the nations! You said in your heart, "I will ascend to the heavens; I will raise my throne above the stars of God; I will sit enthroned on the mount of assembly, on the utmost heights of Mount Zaphon. I will ascend above the tops of the clouds; I will make myself like the Most High." But you are brought down to the realm of the dead, to the depths of the pit. (Isaiah 14:12-15)

Before we dig into what this passage means, we will need to define some of the words used and see where else they are used in Scripture to get a good idea of what they mean.

Go ahead and circle each mention of "morning star," "stars" and "Most High" in the above passage. Stick with me while we define each one:

MORNING STAR, SON OF DAWN: "Morning star" (or "day star") is translated from the Latin word *lucifer*[13] which is another name of Satan.

Please look up Job 38:7 and write it below:

_____

_____

STARS: It's important to recognize that stars are often used in Jewish literature symbolically to refer to angels since both the stars and the angels can in different senses be called 'the hosts of heaven.'" [14]

Please look up Psalm 97:9 and write it below:

_____

_____

MOST HIGH: "Most High" is one of God's names. The Hebrew word *El Elyon* is used in the Hebrew Bible and it means "God Most High" in English.[15]

I've gone ahead and replaced the words that we just studied for your reading convenience. Now read this passage again with the changed wording to help you make sense of it:

> *How you have fallen from heaven, **Satan**! You have been cast down to the earth, you who once laid low the nations! You said in your heart, "I will ascend to the heavens; I will raise my throne above the **angels** of God; I will sit enthroned on the mount of assembly, on the utmost heights of Mount Zaphon. I will ascend above the tops of the clouds; I will make myself like **God**." But you (**Satan**) are brought down to the realm of the dead, to the depths of the pit.* (Isaiah 14:12-15)

When we read this passage, we first see that Satan fell from heaven and was cast down to earth because he wanted to ascend to the heavens and raise his throne above all the angels of God and make himself like God. God was not OK with that and sent him to "the depths of the pit", which means hell.

A certain number of evil angels (called demons) were cast out of heaven with Satan and they now work for Satan doing evil, just like God's angels work for God. Satan and his demons (evil angels) roam the earth.

> *One day the angels came to present themselves before the LORD, and Satan also came with them. The Lord said to Satan, "Where have you come from?" Satan answered the Lord, "From roaming throughout the earth, going back and forth on it." (Job 1:6-7)*

Great. They get thrown out of heaven and now they are left to bother us! But don't worry, God always turns around bad situations and uses them for good. I love that Genesis 50:20 confirms this when it says, "You intended to harm me, but God intended it for good to accomplish what is not being done, the saving of many lives."

Satan was the "brightest" (or highest) angel in heaven, but that wasn't good enough for him. Satan wanted to be like God, but God didn't stand for it and threw him out of heaven. Everything that God can do, Satan tries to counterfeit for his kingdom of darkness. God's kingdom is the kingdom of light and Satan's kingdom is the kingdom of darkness.

Now I want to stop right here with a very important TRUTH! Listen carefully. God's kingdom and Satan's kingdom are NOT equal and they do NOT have equal power. God is the God of the universe and Satan happens to be a part of that. God has all power over Satan and his demons and Satan's time on this earth is limited. There will be a time when Satan and his demons will be thrown into the lake of fire never to return. Because Satan knows his time is short, he and his demons are working as hard as they can to get all people away from God.

Write out Revelation 20:10:

_____

_____

_____

Isn't that great news? Satan will be tormented day and night forever and ever! The bad news is that we need to deal with him until that happens. But the good news is that we serve a God who has ALL power over Satan and when we learn about how our enemy works, we know how to fight him. I can't wait to get into the nuts and bolts about that tomorrow!

Father, I thank You that You have all power over Satan and his demons. I thank You that You want to open my eyes up to the spiritual realm and that You are teaching me how to be aware. I thank You that You are equipping me and teaching me how to fight evil through prayer. I am asking for You to remove all fear of this subject and to give me confidence in You! In Jesus' name, Amen.

Reflection, Notes or Prayer

DAY 1

Day 2

"And lead us not into temptation, but deliver us from the evil one." – Matthew 6:13

SATAN WANTS TO STOP THE CALLING ON YOUR LIFE

When I first stuck my big toe into ministry (ministry as used in Scripture is defined as "one who serves another"[16]) and started to serve God by serving others, everything seemed so hard. I started a little organization where we connected volunteers with needs in our community. I really felt like God had asked me to start this organization and we were helping so many hurting people, BUT IT WAS SO HARD. I had always thought that if God told you to do something and you let Him be in the driver's seat, it would be easy. I mean, if the God who created the universe is on your side, everything should be smooth sailing, right?! Wrong. Just because God asks you to do something doesn't mean it's going to be easy, but it DOES mean that God has so much in store for you and you are going to learn more than you could have ever imagined. The best part of being obedient to God's calling is how close you get to Him. Obedience breeds intimacy with God.

Just a side note about obedience: I've always viewed obedience like a dance. God leads (takes a step) and we follow. He takes another step and we follow. At first the dance moves are simple. We allow Him to lead and we follow and learn the easy stuff. Before we know it, we've gotten into the more difficult but more fun dance moves. God leads us around and obedience just becomes second nature.

So if obedience brings you closer to God and you learn a ton and you get to serve Him in amazing ways, why was this ministry so hard? The problem was that I had no knowledge of spiritual warfare. In fact, I will never forget bawling on the phone to one of my closest friends. I was telling her how hard this ministry was and how nothing seemed to click and how someone was always against what I was trying to do. After I finished crying in her ear, she very calmly said to me, "Angela, you have a target on your back." WHAT?! My tears dried up quickly at the thought that

I had a target on my back. "What in the world are you talking about?" I fired back at her. She asked if I was available to meet for lunch. Over lunch she handed me a book called *Dressed To Kill* by Rick Renner[17] and told me to read it. For the next three days I tore through that book. I couldn't stop reading it. I took pages and pages of notes. I read through the night. I couldn't put the book down. That book addressed so many of the problems that I was facing. I had finally gotten an answer to why everything was so hard.

Satan was trying to stop me from the work that God had called me to do!

Many Christians believe that they are immune from any attacks or schemes of the enemy because they are a follower of Jesus Christ. But I would argue that the opposite is true. Christians are MORE a target of the enemy because we are a threat to his kingdom of darkness. 1 Peter 5:8 says, "Be alert and of sober mind. Your enemy the devil prowls around like a roaring lion looking for someone to devour." I love the Message translation of this verse. It says:

> *Keep a cool head. Stay alert. The Devil is poised to pounce, and would like nothing better than to catch you napping. Keep your guard up. You're not the only ones plunged into these hard times.* ***It's the same with Christians all over the world****. (emphasis mine) So keep a firm grip on the faith. The suffering won't last forever. It won't be long before this generous God who has great plans for us in Christ—eternal and glorious plans they are!—will have you put together and on your feet for good. He gets the last word; yes, he does.* (MSG)

Satan has an agenda.
1. He wants to stop Christians from spreading the good news of Jesus Christ.
2. He wants to grow his kingdom of darkness.
3. He wants to hold people back from the calling God has for them.

4. He wants to hold people back from using the individual gifts God has given each of them.

I imagine that some of you are quaking in your boots about now. I am here to tell you that you have absolutely nothing to be afraid of! Friends, please hear me say that walking with God and serving Him is the biggest joy of my life. The intimacy and love shared by us and the Father as we walk through hard things supersedes anything that Satan can throw at us. God has the VICTORY over Satan. Yes, Satan has an agenda, but God's agenda is bigger and more powerful. God uses Satan and his tactics to draw us closer to Himself. Think about it. Think about the last hard time you went through. Did it draw you closer to God? Did it make you rely on God more than you had in the past? Did it foster a deeper relationship with God? As I mentioned before, one of my very favorite Bible verses is Genesis 50:20 (NKJV). "You meant evil against me; but God meant it for good!" Isn't that exciting? God will use evil for *HIS* good! The story of Joseph is a perfect example.

I challenge you to read Joseph's story in Genesis 37-45 during your quiet time this week or next.

Satan cannot read your mind!! Grudem says that "we should not think that demons can know the future or that they can read our minds or know our thoughts."[18] God knows our thoughts (Psalm 139:2b), but Satan does not. The enemy does not know your thoughts, but he can suggest ideas to see if you will believe him. I'll explain it like this. Do you have that one person in your life who loves to push your buttons? It could be a sibling, spouse, child, or friend. This person knows you really well and knows how to get a rise out of you. They love to push your buttons and get you off track. Do you know that Satan does the same thing? He will try and distract you with those things that will push your buttons and get you off track.

As I was preparing for this study, I happened to stumble on an entry in one of my journals. At the time of this entry I was feeling very defeated. I felt that God placed a dream in my heart to teach and pray for people on a large scale. I poured out all of the thoughts and voices that were in my head at the time. I know I'm showing my dirty laundry to all of you, but I feel like I need to share this to help you identify the kinds of lies that we listen to and agree with. Do you see how believing lies can keep us from the destiny that God has for us?

You are a poor leader

You can't do this

This is all your idea, not God's

God doesn't have plans for you

You are wasting your time

You are going to have to wait forever

You think too highly of yourself

Nobody wants to listen to you

You look like a crazy person to everyone

You're only a mom and you haven't even done that right

You've messed up your kids

So much was going on in my head, I just needed to get it out. After writing all of it down, I quickly realized that those things are not things that God would be speaking to me. I was able to identify them as the voice of the enemy. See how the enemy works? Do you see how he tries to make you stop? How he uses our thoughts to try and defeat us? At that point in my life, I was feeling very defeated. If we don't know that there is an enemy trying to drop these misleading thoughts into our minds, we start to agree with them and find ourselves trapped in the enemy's lies. It debilitates us and stops us from moving forward unless we convert those lies into God's truths. Let me show you how to do this by taking some of the lies listed above and turning them into truths:

Lies	God's Truth (AFFIRMATIONS)
You are a poor leader	*The Spirit of the Sovereign Lord is on me, because the Lord has anointed me to proclaim good news to the poor* (Isaiah 61:1).
God doesn't have plans for me	*God has plans to prosper me and not to harm me, to give me a hope and a future* (Jeremiah 29:11).
You think too highly of yourself	*God opposes the proud but shows favor to the humble* (James 4:6).
You look like a crazy person to everyone	*I am the apple of God's eye* (Psalm 17:8).
You've messed up your kids	*The Lord will teach my children and they will enjoy great peace* (Isaiah 54:13).

It's so important to be using God's truth to combat the lies we listen to. There are times in my life that I have made a chart like the one above and have had to remind myself daily of God's truth. I call them "daily affirmations". Instead of tearing myself up daily, I CHOOSE to affirm myself daily with God's truths!

Now it's your turn. Write down any lies that come to your mind under the "Lies" column and then google Scripture and write an affirmation under the "God's Truth" column.

Lies	God's Truth (AFFIRMATIONS)

The good news is that by knowing how Satan works, we can defend ourselves. Once a thought has come into our mind that would normally send us into a rage of fear, despair, anger, guilt, or condemnation, we can recognize who is sending that thought and we can CHOOSE not only to reject it but also to turn our attention to God and what He says! We can then write out affirmations of God's truths to overcome the lies.

Had I not learned about spiritual warfare, I would have stopped ministry years ago and I would not have been able to experience the true calling that God has for me. Walking in obedience is not always easy, but when we are aware of our opponent, we have a fighting chance!

Take some time to think about the dreams that God has placed on your heart. Write them in the space below.

_____

_____

_____

_____

_____

Now think about the ways the enemy has tried to stop you from pursuing the calling that God has for your life. Write down whatever comes to mind. After writing down all that comes to mind, ask God to forgive you for falling into Satan's traps and ask God for a second chance.

_____

_____

_____

_____

_____

Father, thank You for opening my eyes up to the plans and schemes of the enemy over my life. Forgive me for falling into Satan's traps and stopping when I've known that You've told me to go. Thank You for new eyes to see and new ears to hear. Release me into the plans and calling that You have for my life! In Jesus' name, Amen.

Reflection, Notes or Prayer

Day 3

"And lead us not into temptation, but deliver us from the evil one." – Matthew 6:13

HOW TO IDENTIFY SATAN'S WORK

When we start to look at our troubles and our roadblocks with the awareness that the enemy may be trying to disrupt our plans, it changes the way we see everything. This doesn't mean that we can blame everything bad that happens to us on Satan, but we can't rule him out. WE NEED TO BE AWARE.

The enemy would love to take credit for all that is bad in the world because it makes him look more powerful than he really is. We can't go around thinking that there is a demon around every corner. Bad things happen because of the enemy, but bad things also happen because we live in a fallen world with many, many generations before us tainted with brokenness and sin. In addition to generations of sin, our free will—our ability to act on our own discretion to make our own choices—also plays into bad things happening.

So how do we discern or tell the difference between when the enemy is causing us havoc and when we are just suffering the consequences of living in a fallen world? The truth is that we can't always tell. And ultimately the cause doesn't matter because the solution is still the same. We need to pray. We need to recognize our thoughts. We need to identify the source of whatever thoughts we are believing. As I've mentioned before, we hear three different voices: we hear the voice of God, we hear the voice of the enemy, and we hear our own voice. Our job is to recognize which voice we are heeding. We do that by lining up what we are hearing with the Word of God. (When I say the Word of God, I always mean Scripture.) If we are hearing a voice that is contrary to the Word of God or His character, we can be assured that we are either listening to ourselves or the enemy. Friends, this is why it is soooooooo important that we are reading our Bibles. How can we line up the voices in our head with the Word of God if we don't know the Word of God?

Once again, I never want to come across as legalistic, but when we are reading the Bible every day, we are filling our mind with God's truth and we begin to have the mind of Christ! Having the mind of Christ is so invaluable in this day and age. We want to live our lives seeing everything around us through the eyes of Christ.

God had recently given me a vision about this very topic. He showed me a picture of a giant bubble. Inside the bubble were written all sorts of words, warnings, and decrees that Scripture gives us. The bubble represents a bubble of His protection around us. When we go outside this bubble of His protection, we are then in enemy territory. When we make choices that are going against His Word and commands, we open ourselves up to the kingdom of darkness and Satan's schemes. We have opened a door to allow the enemy access to our minds and our lives.

This may all sound confusing, but let me share with you what Satan uses to make our lives miserable. The enemy uses anything that can be used for darkness such as fear, anxiety, worry, pornography, sexual sin, anger, witchcraft (cults, mediums, channeling, worshipping angels, Ouija board, fortune tellers, tarot cards, spiritualism, new age), abandonment, rejection, despair, insecurity, unworthiness, hate, self-hate, alcoholism, drug abuse, addiction, gossip, slander, envy, bitterness, and so much more.

When we begin to realize that those things the enemy uses for darkness are outside of the bubble of God's protection, we become aware of the things we need to stay away from. If we are dealing with any of these things, Jesus is right there waiting for you to confess and ask for forgiveness. The enemy tries to convince us that there is no hope to break free. His main goal is to have us in a place of bondage outside of that bubble so that he has access to our lives. The good news is that once we admit that we have sinned and we turn away from that sin, the enemy no longer has access to us in that area and WE ARE FREE! Free to enjoy all good things that are from God ("every good and perfect gift is from above" James 1:17)—which includes love, joy, peace, patience, kindness, goodness, faithfulness, gentleness, and self-control, the fruit of God's spirit (Galatians 5:22).

I want to share with you an example of how sneaky the enemy can be in trying to get you outside the bubble of God's protection. In Week 1 of this study, I introduced you to my momma. She is an amazing woman and has followed God her whole life. He saved her from a very rough start in life and has been the Father that she so desperately needed. Two years ago when my father and younger brother passed away eight days apart, God was with my mom in a way that brought her tremendous peace and comfort through that time. She was doing extraordinarily well after their passing and she gives all credit to God. Then a couple of months ago, she mentioned to me that she had been missing my dad and went to see a medium hoping she might be comforted by the experience. Now although my mom had been a very strong believer all those years, she had only read the Bible once when she was 14 years old. She never wanted to do anything outside the will of God, but she didn't know that she was outside the will of God because she wasn't studied in God's Word.

Let's see what Scripture says about mediums:

Leviticus 20:6

_____

_____

Isaiah 8:19

_____

_____

Friends, we need to know God's Word! You'll be happy to know that after I showed my mom the truth in Scripture, she has been on fire for reading the Bible. She reads at *least* an hour a day and she can't get enough of it. Once again, what the enemy meant for evil in my mom's life, God turned around for her good!

As I've said before, I prayed with many people who were in bondage to the schemes of the enemy. Through prayer (mostly confession and forgiveness) I've seen them set completely free! It's absolutely one of the highest honors to watch Jesus set people free right before my eyes. This stuff is real, friends! I've experienced it over and over and over in *my* life and in the lives of others. Through prayer WE CAN BE SET FREE. We just need to know who and what we are fighting against. Isn't that exciting? Don't you feel so much hope right about now? There is hope for you. You were not just *born* to worry. You were not *born* insecure. You were not *born* unworthy. You were not *born* controlling. As long as the enemy can convince you that that's just the way you are, you will continue to be in bondage.

That's it for today! It's been a heavy day, but one that will change how you see things. Let's pray.

Father, thank You for opening up my eyes to the schemes of the enemy. I want to be free. Set me free from any hold of darkness over me. I want You to have access to my whole heart. Show me where You want to set me free and then give me the courage to walk out my freedom with You! In Jesus' name, Amen.

Reflection, Notes or Prayer

Day 4

"And lead us not into temptation, but deliver us from the evil one." – Matthew 6:13

PROTECTING YOURSELF AGAINST THE ENEMY

So now that our eyes have been opened to spiritual warfare, what can we do to protect ourselves from the enemy?

<u>Read the Bible and memorize Scripture.</u> I will never stop saying how important this is! We have to know what Scripture says. It's as important as breathing. I KNOW how hard this is, but it's the hard things that have the most payoff. Just read it. Don't stress yourself out trying to memorize the whole thing. Just read it. As you read it and read it and read it, verses will become familiar to you and you will have some memorized before you know it. So how will reading and memorizing Scripture help you?

1. *The Word of God (Scripture) is the "sword of the Spirit" (Ephesians 6:17).* It's the offensive weapon that God has given us to fight the enemy. The enemy flees when Scripture is read. Just last night, I was alone in my bed (I've taken some time alone to write this study) and I was awakened in complete terror. I immediately knew to call out to Jesus and quote Scripture. I was so overtaken by fear that the only Scripture I could call to mind was the Lord's Prayer!! I said it over and over until peace entered the room.

   Remember that in this week's video I read Matthew 4:1-11. Open your Bible and re-read this passage to jog your memory.

   Jesus used Scripture to fight off Satan. Do you see the three words Jesus said before answering Satan? I'll help you out. Each time Jesus said, "It is written..." and then *quoted Scripture.* Satan eventually fled and left Jesus. We can use the same technique!

2. *The Word of God leads you to truth.* Remember the example with my mom and the medium? We need to know what the Word says so we can stay within God's bubble of protection. We need to know what the Word says so that the enemy can't deceive us with his lies. When we are hearing voices in our heads, we need to know what God's Word says so that we can discern which voice to listen to.

__Pray.__ We fight the enemy through prayer, using Scripture just like Jesus did: to combat the schemes of the enemy. Someone once illustrated the power of quoting Scripture in our prayers by describing God's Word and prayer each as sticks of dynamite. When we put the two together, it's double the explosion! Pray powerfully over the schemes of the enemy using prayers filled with Scripture.

1. *When unsure how to start, learn from authors who are skilled in Scripture-based prayers.*

    Prayers That Avail Much – Anniversary Edition (Germaine Copeland)[19]

    The Power of a Praying...Parent/for Adult Children/ Woman/Husband, etc. (Stormie Omartian)[20]

    Praying God's Word: Breaking Free from Spiritual Strongholds (Beth Moore)[21]

2. *Pray the full armor of God (Ephesians 6:10-17) over your-selves and those you love.* I try to do this every morning. This passage teaches us how to put on the *spiritual armor* that God provides us for protection against the enemy.

3. *Pray and confess your sins and any unforgiveness every day.* When we are holding onto these things, we are outside God's bubble of protection. Pray and ask God to reveal any sins or unforgiveness that need to be uncovered.

4. *Take control over your thought life.* Think about what you think about. If I catch myself entertaining temptation or lies, I simply say out loud, "Not today, Satan!" With that state-ment I remind myself that I don't have to listen to those voices. I will choose what God has to say!

5. *Praise God through your prayers.* Remember in our Week 1, Day 4 homework when I told you the story about my son getting a talking-to from my husband? Remember when I said I made a conscious choice to praise God instead of going down the bunny trail of fear and worry? Friends, we can't be praising God and listening to the enemy at the same time. Notice how we have come full circle from the begin-ning of the study. Praising God is such an important part of prayer and such an important tool to fight off the enemy! __Everything starts and ends with praising God. If you get that down, the only way to go with God is deeper!__

Stay humble. Remember that pride is what got Satan kicked out of heaven and pride is one of the enemy's favorite strategies against us. If we think about ourselves over focusing on God, pride has done its job. When we are focused on me, me, me, we lose the heavenly perspective. Most people view pride as elevating oneself over others, but pride also exists at the opposite end of the spectrum. When we despair or consider ourselves below others, we are also operating in pride because we are focusing on ourselves. Both perspectives make ourselves the center. At all times, we want to make God the one we focus on, not ourselves.

> There are several Scriptures on both pride and humility. Look up these Scriptures and mark the ones that speak to you.
>
> James 4:6
> Jeremiah 9:23-24
> 1 John 2:16
> 2 Corinthians 10:12
> Deuteronomy 8:2-3
> Galatians 6:3-4
> Isaiah 2:12
> Philippians 2:3
> Proverbs 8:13
> Proverbs 11:2

Learn about spiritual warfare. Don't shy away from it. Some people think it's scary, but I think it's scary not to know what you are up against! I would highly recommend Rick Renner's book *Dressed to Kill* if you want to dive deeper.

Well, friends—we made it! We made it through the Lord's Prayer as it is in Matthew 6:9-13. My prayer for you is that you will never look at this prayer the same and that you will use it as a structure to pray. I also pray that your eyes have been opened to the need for prayer in your life, not just to ask for something, but to praise God, to pray for others, to pray for ourselves, to confess our sins, and to pray powerful prayers that hold back the enemy.

There have been times in my journey with God that I have neglected spending time with Him in daily prayer. In those times I have felt distant from Him, like I can't hear His voice. Like I'm not sensing the direction that He is leading. Please do not neglect spending time in prayer. Set your alarm clock ten minutes earlier.

Give God the best part of your day and watch how the intimacy between you and Him grows!

Join me as I wrap up this study in Video 6. Bless you, friends!

Father, I thank You for my new friends in Christ. I thank You for being such an awesome teacher, for opening our eyes to how much prayer entails and to the power it has! We pray that we will never look at the Lord's Prayer the same and that our relationship and intimacy with You would grow through following this structure of prayer. Thank You for teaching us how to pray. We love You!

Our Father in heaven,
hallowed be Your name.
Your kingdom come,
Your will be done,
on earth as it is in heaven.
Give us today our daily bread.
And forgive us our debts,
as we also have forgiven our debtors.
And lead us not into temptation,
but deliver us from the evil one.

In Jesus' name, Amen

Reflection, Notes or Prayer

_____

_____

_____

_____

_____

_____

_____

_____

Week Six

Week of Review

Video Six

(To watch *Video Six*, go to angelaackley.com)

Watch Video Six and use this space to take notes. You may want to jot down Scriptures that speak to you or any comments or stories that you don't want to forget!

_____

_____

_____

_____

_____

_____

_____

_____

_____

_____

_____

_____

_____

_____

_____

_____

_____

_____

I'm so glad you've gathered a group to journey through ***Jesus, Help Me Pray!***. Please plan to meet together six consecutive weeks, scheduling each meeting to run anywhere from an hour and a half to two hours, depending on how long you would like the discussion to last.

Make everyone feel welcomed!

As I've learned from the many group Bible studies I've led and attended over the years, it's so important to make sure that everyone in your group feels welcomed, included, and LOVED! For some people, it takes great courage to sign up for a study with strangers. One thing that I love to do at the first meeting (and sometimes even the second) is ask those who don't know anybody to raise their hands. I then ask everyone surrounding that person to tell them that ***they are loved*** and that ***they are glad they are there***. Please feel free to do the same. Everyone needs to feel like they belong!

Confidentiality

In addition to making everyone feel welcomed, please communicate that this is a confidential group. What is said in the group, stays in the group. Also, please communicate that this is a **no-judgment** zone, that we are not going to judge anyone or rank anyone based on how far along they are in their prayer life or their relationship with God.

Homework

First, please assure attendees that homework is ***not a requirement*** to come to the gatherings and that we never want anyone to feel like they can't attend a gathering if they didn't finish their homework! Mention to attendees that when they are going through the homework each week, they should circle or highlight anything that would make a good topic of discussion. Encourage them to share their highlights during discussion.

Weekly Format

This study includes both videos and homework. At the first gathering, it's important to communicate what each week will look like so attendees will know what is expected of them. Each week's meeting will entail a video (watched as a group) and two sets of discussion questions (one about the video and one about the previous week's homework).

To help guide your time together and make planning easier, each week is outlined in detail and the length of each video is provided. Discussion questions are in **bold**.

Week One

- Open in prayer.
- *Ice Breaker.* If possible, provide a piece of cardstock (half sheet or quarter sheet works best) for each person in the group. Provide different color markers if you have some available. Welcome your group and open by asking each person to google the meaning of their name. Once they have the meaning, have them write their name and the meaning of their name (in large print, with or without colored markers) on a piece of cardstock. Break into groups of 6-8 and share with each other your name and meaning. Encourage everyone to keep their piece of paper as a bookmark or to display it somewhere as a reminder.
- Play Video One (32:48).
- Post-video discussion questions:
  1. **Does anyone want to share something that stood out to you in the video?**
  2. **What are you hoping to learn from this study?**
  3. **Do you already praise God in your prayer time? If so, what does praising God look like for you?**
  4. **Which of the following words/phrases would you use to describe your prayer life:**
     a. **Needs Improvement**
     b. **Mediocre**
     c. **Fruitful**
- Close in prayer. Ask that God would take all of our prayer lives to a fruitful place as we embark on this study of prayer.

Week Two

- Open in prayer.
- Discuss last week's study (Week One homework):
  1. **Does anyone want to share something that stood out to you last week?**
  2. **Which method of praising God was new for you?**
  3. **Can you think of a time when you chose to praise God instead of worrying?**

4. **How can you use praising God as a tool to keep your eyes fixed on God instead of on yourself and your circumstances?**

- Play Video Two (35:23).
- Post-video discussion questions:
    1. **Does anyone want to share something that you circled or highlighted last week?**
    2. **Did anyone feel the prompting to accept Jesus into your heart?** *(If so, have someone pray for that person!)*
    3. **Did God lay anyone on your heart that you need to start praying for?**
    4. Ask members of the group if they need prayer for anything. Encourage the group to be lifting each other up in prayer. When asked for a prayer request, group members often will share a prayer request for a family member or friend and not for themselves. Encourage group members to share a *personal* prayer request by saying, "*I just want everyone to know that I truly love your family and friends, but I really want to pray for YOU.*"
- Close in prayer.

Week Three

- Open in prayer.
- Discuss last week's study (Week Two homework):
    1. **Does anyone want to share something that you circled or highlighted last week?**
    2. **Can you share a time that you prayed for someone and you saw God move?**
    3. **What are some of the things that you have learned by praying for people?**
- Play Video Three (43:17).
- Post-video discussion questions:
    1. **Does anyone want to share something that stood out to you in the video?**
    2. **Do you have difficulty praying for yourself? Have you ever stopped to consider that this difficulty is actually sending the message to God that we *can* and *should* take care of ourselves?** *After discussing this question, stop and offer a prayer of repentance as a group for thinking that we would know better how to take care of ourselves over how God wants to take care of us.*

3. Angela talked about surrendering all areas of our lives to God so that He can feed us. What do you have the most trouble surrendering to God? *After everyone has shared, pray as a group and ask God to help each person fully surrender to Him.*

• Close in prayer.

Week Four

• Open in prayer.
• Discuss last week's study (Week Three homework):
   1. Does anyone want to share something that you circled or highlighted last week?
   2. Did everyone have a chance to dedicate (or consecrate) your bodies to Jesus? What did you think of the experience?
   3. Our soul is made up of our mind, our will, and our emotions. Which of the three are you most needing Jesus to fill?
• Play Video Four (40:27).
• Post-video discussion questions:
   1. Does anyone want to share something that stood out to you in the video?
   2. Angela talked about the difference between "conviction" and "condemnation." Conviction is when the Holy Spirit convicts us of our wrong and condemnation is when the enemy continually hits us over the head with our wrongs. Can you share a time when you have been either convicted of or condemned by your sin?
   3. Did God bring someone to mind that you need to forgive? *As a group, this would be an appropriate time to pray for the person that needs to forgive.*
   4. How are you feeling knowing that we are going to be walking into a week of study talking about forgiveness?
• Close in prayer. Ask God for courage and boldness for everyone as they start their week of confession.

Week Five

- Open in prayer.
- Discuss last week's study (Week Four homework):
  1. **Does anyone want to share something that you circled or highlighted last week?**
  2. **What part of confession had the greatest impact on you: forgiving someone, being forgiven, forgiving yourself, or recognizing lies that you've believed?**
  3. **Does anyone want to share a story of freedom that you experienced through doing the homework?**
- Play Video Five (49:23).
- Post-video discussion questions:
  1. **Does anyone want to share something that stood out to you in the video?**
  2. **Are you familiar with the "full armor of God" described in Ephesians 6:10-18?**
  3. **How have you applied the full armor of God in your own life?**
- Encourage group members to share a personal testimony of the power of prayer at your next meeting.
- Close in prayer.

Week Six

- Open in prayer.
- Discuss last week's study (Week Five homework):
  1. **Does anyone want to share something that you circled or highlighted last week?**
  2. **Of all that you learned about spiritual warfare, what had the greatest impact on you?**
  3. **Knowing the Word of God is so important in keeping us on the right path. How do you incorporate reading the Bible into your day?**
- Play Video Six (13:33).
- Post-video discussion questions:
  1. **Does anyone want to share something that stood out to you in the video?**

2. How has your prayer life changed as a result of this study?
3. *Upward*: Have you seen any value in praising God?
4. *Outward*: Have you been challenged to pray for others in person?
5. *Inward*: As you learned to pray inward, what are some things God has revealed to you that you need to let go of?
6. *Confession*: Have you seen the value of confession?
7. *Spiritual Warfare*: How have your prayers changed as they relate to spiritual warfare?

- Invite anyone to share a personal testimony of the power of prayer.
- Close in prayer.

Bibliography

Butler, Trent C. *Holman Illustrated Bible Dictionary*. Nashville: Holman Bible Publishers, 2003.

Copeland, Germaine. *Prayers That Avail Much: 25th Anniversary Edition*. Tulsa: Harrison House, 1997.

Dean, Jennifer Kennedy. *Live A Praying Life-Anniversary Edition*. Birmingham: New Hope Publishers, 2010.

Grudem, Wayne. *Systematic Theology: An Introduction To Biblical Doctrine*. Grand Rapids: Zondervan, 1994.

Hunt, June. *Counseling Through Your Bible Handbook: Providing Biblical Hope and Practical Help for Everyday Problems*. Eugene: Harvest House Publishers, 2008.

Moore, Beth. *Praying God's Word: Breaking Free from Spiritual Strongholds*. Nashville: B&H Publishing Group, 2009.

Omartian, Stormie. *Power of a Praying Parent*. Eugene: Harvest House Publishers, 2014.

Omartian, Stormie. *Prayer Warrior: The Power of Praying Your Way to Victory*. Eugene: Harvest House Publishers, 2013.

Renner, Rick. *Dressed To Kill*. Tulsa: Harrison House, 1991.

Shirer, Priscilla. *Discerning The Voice of God: How To Recognize When God Speaks*. Nashville: Lifeway Press, 2017.

Willard, Dallas and Simpson, Don. *Revolution of Character: Discovering Christ's Pattern for Spiritual Transformation*. Colorado Springs: Navpress, 2005.

Endnotes

WEEK ONE

1. Merriam-Webster Dictionary, accessed September 9, 2021, s.v. "hallowed."

WEEK TWO

2. Jennifer Kennedy Dean, *Live A Praying Life – Anniversary Edition* (Birmingham: New Hope Publishers, 2010), 47.
3. Dean, *Live*, 27.
4. Butler, Trent C., *Holman Illustrated Bible Dictionary* (Nashville: Holman Bible Publishers, 2003), 828.
5. Germaine Copeland, *Prayers That Avail Much: 25th Anniversary Edition* (Tulsa: Harrison House, 1997).
6. Stormie Omartian, *Power of a Praying Parent (Eugene: Harvest House Publishers, 2014).*

WEEK FOUR

7. Google dictionary, accessed August 27, 2021, s.v. "confession."
8. Google dictionary, accessed August 27, 2021, s.v. "deliverance."

WEEK FIVE

9. "Spiritual Warfare", Wikipedia, accessed August 27, 2021, https://en.wikipedia.org/wiki/Spiritual_warfare.
10. Wayne Grudem, *Systematic Theology: An Introduction To Biblical Doctrine*, (Grand Rapids: Zondervan, 1994).
11. Grudem, *Systematic*, 412-3.
12. Grudem, *Systematic*, 413.
13. Butler, *Holman*, 398.

14.   Matt Slick, "Where in the Bible Does it Say That One-Third of the Angels Fell?" CARM, Aug 9, 2009, https://carm.org/about-angels/where-in-the-bible-does-it-say-that-one-third-of-the-angels-fell/.

15.   Trent C. Butler, *Holman Illustrated Bible Dictionary* (Nashville: Holman Bible Publishers, 2003), 1172.

16.   Butler, *Holman* , 1134.

17.   Rick Renner, *Dressed To Kill,* (Tulsa: Harrison House, 1991).

18.   Grudem, *Systematic* , 416.

19.   Germaine Copeland. *Prayers That Avail Much: 25th Anniversary Edition* (Tulsa: Harrison House, 1997).

20.   Stormie Omartian, *Power of a Praying Parent* (Eugene: Harvest House Publishers, 2014).

21.   Beth Moore, *Praying God's Word: Breaking Free from Spiritual Strongholds* (Nashville: B&H Publishing Group, 2009).

CPSIA information can be obtained
at www.ICGtesting.com
Printed in the USA
LVHW072158210222
711655LV00016B/623

9 781662 836152